GLACIER COUNTRY

MONTANA'S GLACIER NATIONAL PARK

— Revised Edition —

by R.C. "Bert" Gildart,

David Alt, C.W. Buchholtz, and Bob Frauson

FARCOUNTRY PRESS

Medicine Grizzly Lake viewed from above. JOHN LAMBING

ISBN: 978-1-56037-811-2

Design by Steph Lehmann

Front cover photo: Wild Goose Island is a focal point on Saint Mary Lake. PHOTOGRAPH BY ZACK CLOTHIER.
Back cover photo: Grinnell Lake beneath Angel Wing. PHOTOGRAPH BY ZACK CLOTHIER.
Title page photo: Beargrass blooming along Going-to-the-Sun Road. PHOTOGRAPH BY CHUCK HANEY.

FARCOUNTRY PRESS

For more information about our books, write Farcountry Press, P.O. Box 5630, Helena, MT 59604; call (800) 821-3874; or visit www.farcountrypress.com.

Produced and printed in the United States of America.

26 25 24 23 23 1 2 3 4 5

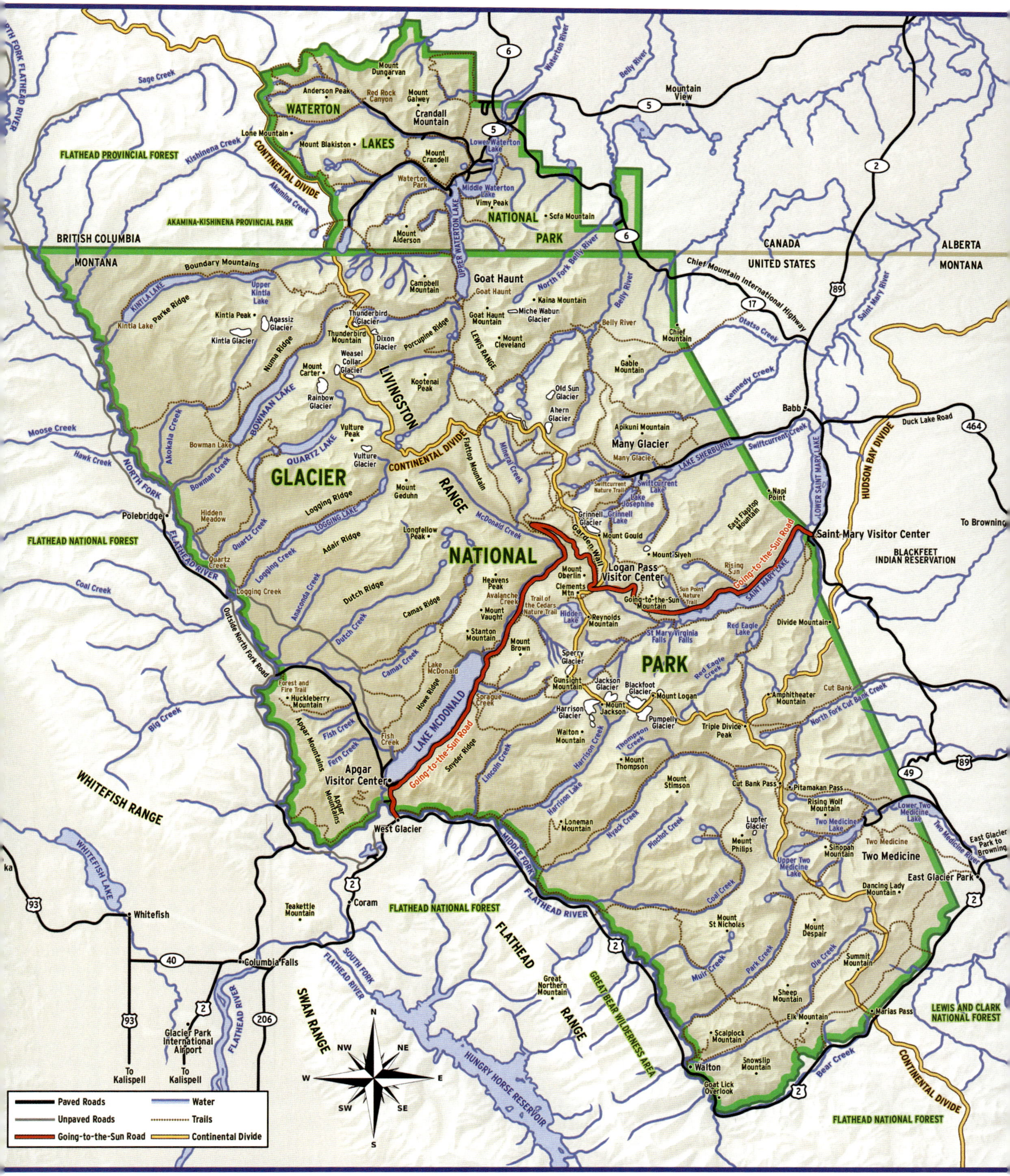

WATERTON
LAKES
NATIONAL
PARK
GLACIER
NATIONAL
PARK
LIVINGSTON
RANGE
LEWIS RANGE
CONTINENTAL DIVIDE
BRITISH COLUMBIA
ALBERTA
MONTANA
CANADA
UNITED STATES
FLATHEAD PROVINCIAL FOREST
AKAMINA-KISHINENA PROVINCIAL PARK
FLATHEAD NATIONAL FOREST
LEWIS AND CLARK NATIONAL FOREST
BLACKFEET INDIAN RESERVATION
WHITEFISH RANGE
SWAN RANGE
FLATHEAD RANGE
GREAT BEAR WILDERNESS AREA
HUNGRY HORSE RESERVOIR
LAKE MCDONALD
Going-to-the-Sun Road
Logan Pass Visitor Center
Apgar Visitor Center
Saint Mary Visitor Center
West Glacier
Polebridge
Whitefish
Columbia Falls
Coram
Babb
Walton
East Glacier Park
Two Medicine
Many Glacier
Goat Haunt
To Kalispell
To Browning
Glacier Park International Airport
Chief Mountain International Highway
Paved Roads
Unpaved Roads
Going-to-the-Sun Road
Water
Trails
Continental Divide

Garden Wall wildflowers. ZACK CLOTHIER

Contents

Grizzly bears can be observed by lucky park visitors—at a safe distance. BERT GILDART

Mountain goats grazing below Bearhat Mountain. JOHN LAMBING

Welcome to Glacier Country

GLACIER NATIONAL PARK CAN BE APPROACHED FROM ALL FOUR POINTS OF THE COMPASS, but the eastern approach is the one that is particularly inspiring. From this direction, along U.S. Highway 2 through the prairies of eastern Montana, there is little hint of the vast mountain ranges that loom ahead. Not until you are within about fifty miles and suddenly rise from the depth of a coulee will you see that what appeared to be clouds glimmering on the horizon are in fact lofty mountains shrouded in snow and ice.

Some 230 years ago, when this range was first seen by Euro-Americans, adventurers were prompted to call this the "land of shining mountains." Today, this area could be called the land of glorious adversity, for contemporary scientists tell us that the park was born of fire, quenched by torrential rains, inundated by vast seas, forced upward by internal pressures, and then gouged by great continental ice sheets that came and went on at least four occasions. From this heritage, mountains were molded that touch the sky and cradle more than 200 lakes. Such is the legacy the eons left for some 71 species of mammals, 276 of birds, and 1,200 of plants that now inhabit the 1,583 square miles of Glacier National Park.

Glacier's features can be enjoyed with drink in hand from a recliner on the terrace of one of the park's four magnificent lodges, from the deck of a lake-skimming launch, or by bus, car, bicycle, horseback, or on foot. Personal tastes determine how to spend the time, and so it is advisable to become acquainted with the park's generalized features as quickly as possible. The National Park Service is prepared to assist in a number of ways. Near each entrance is either an information center or an elaborate visitor center. Here, rangers and naturalists are available to acquaint travelers with the various types of accommodations and interpretive programs. In addition, displays assist interpretation and to guide the curious to places of interest.

At first encounter, the park may appear a forbidding place to explore, but this is not the case. It is bisected by the famed Going-to-the-Sun Road, which provides motorists with numerous pullovers for introductions to various features. Park shuttle buses and guided tour buses provided by park concessionaires relieve motorists of driving.

After this introductory tour, many visitors are inspired to explore on foot. Almost 700 miles of trail await the hiker, extending from low forested hills up to boulder-strewn passes. Reached by several of these trails, two back-country chalets cater to hikers who do not want to carry heavy packs. In fact, it isn't necessary to tote anything more than bear deterrent spray, a toothbrush, camera, a jacket, a canteen of water, and a map, as both Granite Park and Sperry Chalets offer food and bedding.

Remote campgrounds provide hikers with nature's own accommodations. Some sites can be reserved online in advance; others are first-come, first-serve with a backcountry permit.

Glacier is a park of incredible natural diversity. Five habitat types occur here, largely determined by weather, which in turn is influenced by altitude. In Glacier, then, it is possible to see grassland, deciduous forest, coniferous forest, alpine tundra, and even the equivalent of polar ice and snow. The habitat changes visitors witness as they rise through Glacier's elevations are similar to what they would see driving thousands of miles north across the United States and Canada.

For those interested in learning about wildlife and the areas where it can be found, it is advisable to learn Glacier's zones. In the spring, for instance, the initiated go to the coniferous forest to find elk, moose, squirrels and chipmunks, and the most cooperative and photogenic dusky grouse. Follow the bird's ventriloquistic hooting to its territory to observe the display of roseate shoulder patches and flaring eye patches as it warns other grouse away.

Perhaps Glacier's most spectacular zone is the arctic-alpine. Here, hardy wildflowers have adapted to this harsh climate in a variety of ways. Some of the flowers are covered with fine hair-like structures that retard evaporation from the desiccating winds. Other plants have overcome these forces by growing in mats and clumps. Almost all are perennials; the short alpine summer doesn't allow enough time for annuals to complete their life cycles.

Despite the adverse conditions of the arctic-alpine zone, this area is home for some of the park's most interesting wildlife. Bighorn sheep may be seen in a variety of locales, but one particularly good spot is midway between Logan Pass and Granite Park Chalet. Interested visitors should leave Logan Pass and hike the Highline Trail. Four miles along, a huge formation juts away from the main ridge of mountain like a flying buttress. This monolith is Haystack Butte; here, in its bracing arch, snow lingers and provides sheep, as well as goats and marmots, with a cool reprieve from the intense alpine sun. July through September is the best time to visit this area as, with the advent of cool weather, all but a few specially adapted species (such as the ptarmigan) either migrate from the arctic-alpine area, or hibernate beneath Glacier's inevitable mantle of winter snow.

This book is an introduction to the general landscape, colorful past, and natural diversity of Glacier National Park, a place which many Americans think of when they envision Montana.

A cloudy Haystack Butte. NPS/JACOB W. FRANK

GEOLOGY

Lake McDonald at sunset beneath the snowy mountains of Glacier National Park. KEVIN LEAGUE

Glaciated Park

by David Alt

GLACIER PARK. IT SHOULD HAVE BEEN CALLED "GLACIATED PARK," because this is a poor place to see modern glaciers and an excellent place to see mountains sculpted by the great ice age glaciers. And an excellent place to see many other things.

Those mountains consist of sedimentary rocks more than 1 billion years old, some of the oldest well-preserved sedimentary rocks in the country. The rocks preserve a record of the Earth as it was before land plants existed, before there were animals of any kind, or atmospheric oxygen that animals might breathe. The record tells of a planet so unfamiliar that it might be another planet, as distant in space as in time.

So 60 million or so years ago, those rocks moved into their present position during the crustal movements that created the Rocky Mountains. Evidence of that movement is clearly visible in the landscape of the eastern part of Glacier Park.

During the last 2 or 3 million years, a succession of great ice ages brought enormous glaciers to North America and northern Europe, and to high mountains all over the world. At least during the last ice age, and presumably during earlier ice ages, an ice cap covered the high areas of Glacier Park, and huge rivers of ice creaked awkwardly down the large canyons, scouring the bedrock and then dumping their loads of eroded sediment farther down the valley.

The grinding rivers of ice melted about 10,000 years ago, leaving their legacy in the craggy peaks and ridges, the deep valleys and the sparkling lakes that make the modern landscape of Glacier Park so magnificently beautiful. Only glaciation on a large scale can bring mountains to such rugged perfection.

The Archives of a Vanished Planet

Almost all the rocks exposed in the cliffs and roadcuts of Glacier Park began as layers of sand, mud, and lime mud deposited a billion or more years ago. Now they are layers of sandstone, mudstone, and limestone. Most of the rocks in the park date from an extremely long interval that geologists call Precambrian time, because it preceded the Cambrian period when the first animals appeared on Earth.

A billion years is a long time, even by the elongated standards of geology, and the Precambrian formations in Glacier Park rank among the oldest well-preserved sedimentary rocks in the country. Like all sedimentary rocks, they contain a record of the environment in which the original sand and mud accumulated. The Precambrian rocks in Glacier Park appear to have formed in an environment unlike any that exists today, unlike any that has existed for hundreds of millions of years. The Earth of a billion years ago had not yet developed into the pleasant and hospitable home we know today.

This is not the place to discuss the subject in detail, but it seems worth mentioning that billion-year-old sedimentary rocks commonly hold evidence of an atmosphere that contained only a trace of oxygen. We would quickly suffocate if we could visit the Earth of that time. Furthermore, the scarcity of atmospheric oxygen would have left the Earth without its ozone layer, which now protects the surface from ultraviolet radiation.

Further evidence in the rocks lead geologists to suspect that the Precambrian atmosphere did contain enormous amounts of carbon dioxide, though this is informed conjecture rather than solid fact. If the ancient atmosphere did indeed include large amounts of carbon dioxide, that would have made the climate hot, because carbon dioxide causes a greenhouse effect. High temperatures, if they existed, would have increased the rate of evaporation from the oceans, and the combination of heat and humidity would have resembled a global sauna bath.

Picture then the shadeless landscape of Precambrian time. The barren land sweltered under heavy clouds and was lifeless except for scummy growths of green algae in shallow pools of water. The seacoast lay somewhere near Glacier Park, probably shifting back and forth as the years passed. Most of the rocks we see in the park appear to have accumulated near that coast, some on land, others in shallow water not very far from land.

The rock formations of Glacier Park are few in number, very thick, and appear as broad bands of distinctive color in the landscape. Anyone can quickly learn to recognize them. Pebbles eroded from those formations make the brightly colored streambeds that so many visitors to the park remember long after they forget some of the more spectacular sights.

The Altyn Limestone

The oldest Precambrian formation in Glacier Park is the Altyn limestone of the eastern mountain front. It tends to be a bit inconspicuous, even though it is about 2,000 feet thick, and is most easily seen around the Many Glacier Hotel and the east end of St. Mary Lake. Altyn limestone is almost white in fresh roadcuts, tan on weathered surfaces, and contains numerous sand grains and small pebbles. It appears to have accumulated in shallow waters, perhaps in seawater, although there is no way to be quite sure of that. The Altyn limestone passes upward into the green and dark gray mudstones of the Appekuny formation.

The Appekuny Mudstone

The Appekuny mudstone is several thousand feet of somber green rock that becomes very dark in the western part of the park. The formation is more than 3,000 feet thick, and it forms a dark gray or greenish-gray band in the landscape. At close range, it is simply layered green rock in the eastern part of the park; in the western part, rock so dark that it is almost black. Any green rock in Glacier Park is almost certainly Appekuny mudstone.

At the top of the Appekuny mudstone, layers of red mudstone begin to appear, and they increase in number upwards. Geologists draw the contact between the Appekuny mudstone and the Grinnell mudstone above it where the red begins to overwhelm the green.

The Grinnell Mudstone

The Grinnell mudstone is about 2,500 feet thick, a broad reddish band in the landscape. Roadcuts of Grinnell mudstone are as red as a freshly painted barn, as they should be, because the same iron oxide pigment colors both. Except in the highest mountains near the middle of the park, any red rock in Glacier Park is likely to be Grinnell mudstone.

Watch the exposures of red mudstone for fossil mudcracks and ripple marks that look as though they were on a modern mudflat at low tide. Similar structures also exist in the green Appekuny formation, although not nearly so abundantly as in the red mudstones. As we look at those ripple marks and mudcracks,

Above: *Reddish mudstone gives a banded appearance to glacier-carved peaks.* ALEXA ZARI/SHUTTERSTOCK

Right: *Stromatolites are the fossils of ancient algae.* BERT GILDART

Below: *Glacial scratches are visual evidence of the geologic past.* HASEG77/SHUTTERSTOCK

we see the remains of rippling pools of shallow water that lay here a billion years ago, and of mudflats that baked hard in the heat. However, geologists cannot be sure whether those pools and mudflats existed near the seashore, along the borders of a desert lake, or perhaps in some obsolete environment that has not existed since Precambrian time.

Both the Appekuny and Grinnell mudstones contain a few beds of white sandstone that make prominent ledges on the hillsides. Some of the most beautiful rock outcrops in the park display bright red Grinnell mudstone and stark white sandstone in vivid contrast.

The Siyeh Limestone

Pale gray cliffs of Siyeh limestone tower above the red Grinnell mudstones to dominate the high country in most of the central part of Glacier Park. The formation is about 3,500 feet thick and, more than any other, is the rock that park visitors see.

Many exposures of Siyeh limestone contain fossil algal structures called "stromatolites" that look almost as though they might be fossil cabbages. Exactly similar structures grow today in a few places, so we know that stromatolites are the remains of extremely primitive blue-green algae. We are all familiar with blue-green algae as the plant that forms scummy growth in puddles, covers the north sides of trees and rocks, and infests fish tanks. Stromatolites range from a few inches to several feet in diameter, and they commonly formed reefs that completely fill entire layers of rock. Some of the ledges of Siyeh limestone around Logan Pass and along the trail to Hidden Lake contain excellent stromatolites. Similar fossils exist locally and less abundantly in the Altyn limestone and the red mudstones. We should all view those fossils with respect and admiration, as early pioneers that led the way for other forms of life. We would not be here now had they not been here then.

Primitive though they are, blue-green algae are green plants that absorb atmospheric carbon dioxide, produce organic matter, and release oxygen to create the kind of air animals can breathe.

Of course, an atom of carbon buried in sedimentary rocks must balance every molecule of oxygen in the atmosphere to account for the original carbon dioxide. The Siyeh limestone is dark in fresh exposure because it contains organic matter, so much in some places that freshly broken rock smells putrid. That billion-year-old odor of decay is one of the reasons that the air we breathe contains oxygen.

The Purcell Diabase Sill

The upper part of the Siyeh formation contains a conspicuous layer about 100 feet thick of black igneous rock called "diabase" sandwiched between layers of limestone. Molten magma squirted between sedimentary layers to form the layer of igneous rock. Geologists call an igneous intrusion formed that way a "sill." Precambrian sedimentary rocks throughout the northern Rocky Mountains contain hundreds of thick sills. This particularly conspicuous and well-known example in Glacier Park is called the Purcell sill.

Heat from the magma drove the dark organic stain out of the Siyeh limestone above and below the sill, bleaching it white. So the sill appears as a nearly horizontal black band bordered in white above and below, a conspicuous striped ribbon on many of the cliffs high in the park. Several roadcuts at the top of Logan Pass expose the Purcell sill, and the Logan Pass end of the trail to Granite Park (the Highline Trail), passes several outstanding exposures of the sill, and of the bleached limestone near its borders.

At Granite Park, the Purcell sill turns into a lava flow of the kind that geologists call pillow basalt. The magma evidently erupted into the water in which the Siyeh limestone was accumulating and formed a pile of

Single Shot Mountain shows the distinctive white-black-white banding of the Purcell diabase sill. JOHN LAMBING

cylindrical masses that look a bit like oversized pillows where we see them exposed in outcrops. Lavas that erupt underwater generally do that.

Age dates obtained by analyzing the radioactive elements in diabase from the Purcell sill show that it is slightly more than 1 billion years old. That must also be the age of the upper part of the Siyeh limestone, because the sill erupted as a lava flow into the formation while it was still soft and muddy. Therefore, all the rocks below the Siyeh limestone must be more than 1 billion years old. We have no better clue to the age of the rocks in the park than the exposures at Granite Park.

Despite the name, there is no granite at Granite Park, or anywhere else in or even near Glacier Park. Even though the diabase of the Purcell sill vaguely resembles granite in that both are speckled igneous rocks, the two rocks differ in most respects. Most obviously, granite is very pale gray, while diabase is very dark gray, almost black in many places. Pieces of diabase from the Purcell sill are common nearly everywhere in the park. Watch the streambeds for pebbles of dark gray rock speckled with light crystals of feldspar about the size of rice grains.

Mount Reynolds and Logan Pass shrouded in wispy clouds. CHUCK HANEY

Shepard and Kintla Formations

The trail from the visitor center at Logan Pass to Hidden Lake is one of the best places to see the Shepard formation, about 1,000 feet of mostly red and tan mudstone. Nearly every outcrop along the higher part of that route is a natural museum of beautiful ripple marks and mudcracks, still exquisitely preserved almost a billion years after they formed. The upper part of the formation blends into about 1,000 feet of red mudstone that geologists call the Kintla formation. Most people look at the Kintla mudstones from a distance because there is no place to see them at close range without a strenuous climb. Look at the red caps on many of the high mountains near the middle of the park.

The Shepard and Kintla formations are the youngest Precambrian rocks in the park. Even they contain no hint of the abundant animal life that would appear on Earth a few hundred million years after they formed. In fact, the perfect preservation of very fine sedimentary details such as ripple marks and mudcracks in these rocks strongly suggests that animals had not yet appeared. In more recent times, digging and crawling animals have generally destroyed such structures long before the original soft sediments could harden into rock.

The Lewis Overthrust Fault

So far as anyone knows, the rocks we see in Glacier Park lay undisturbed until the Rocky Mountains formed sometime around 65 million years ago, give or take 10 million. All sorts of complex things happened as the Rocky Mountains formed, and the details need not concern us here because they do no greatly affect what we see in the park. One event that we do see clearly expressed in the landscape of Glacier Park was movement on the Lewis overthrust fault.

The large slab of Precambrian sedimentary rock that we see in the park slid eastward down a gently sloping surface that geologists call the Lewis overthrust fault. No one knows exactly where the slab of Precambrian sedimentary rock came from, or exactly how far it moved. It must have come at least 35 miles, perhaps as far as 50 miles, conceivably farther. Neither does anyone know how long that movement lasted, but it was certainly not sudden, and probably continued for several million years at an imperceptibly slow pace. The fault appears in the landscape of the eastern part of the park.

At the Lewis overthrust fault, steep hills and cliffs of hard Precambrian rock rise abruptly above a softly rolling landscape eroded on much softer rocks beneath. The line of the fault exactly traces the eastern front of the mountains, where the rugged face of the Rocky Mountains meets the open expanse of the northern high plains. People driving beside St. Mary Lake cross the fault at the narrows near Rising Sun Campground, at a cliff of Altyn limestone.

Precambrian rocks above the Lewis overthrust fault lie on top of Cretaceous brown sandstones and black mudstones only about 100 million years old, the same rocks that lie beneath the high plains east of the park. The Cretaceous rocks below the Lewis overthrust fault accumulated in shallow seawater at the western margin of an inland sea that then flooded much of central North America. Animal fossils do exist in the Cretaceous rocks, but they are hard to find because these rocks weather easily and form very few good exposures.

The Lewis overthrust fault reverses the normal state of affairs in which the youngest rocks lie at the top of the stack, the oldest at the bottom. Glacier Park was one of the first places geologists found overthrust faults of this kind back in the 1890s, and it remains among the best places to see an overthrust fault. The best way to obtain a grand view of the Lewis overthrust fault is to look north from the top of Marias Pass on U.S. Highway 2 at the mountains in the southern edge of the park. You can see the tan Altyn limestone just above the fault as a straight band of tan rock that slopes like a railway grade descending to the west.

We see the Lewis overthrust fault best expressed in Chief Mountain, a block of Precambrian sedimentary rock isolated by erosion from the rest of the overthrust slab. On all sides of Chief Mountain, the hard Precambrian sedimentary rocks rise in steep cliffs above the much softer Cretaceous sedimentary rocks that surround the mountain and continue beneath it.

Chief Mountain, the park's best example of the Lewis Overthrust.
KEVIN LEAGUE

Kintla Lake is located in the North Fork region of the park. NPS

North Fork Valley

We see another aspect of the Lewis overthrust fault in the North Fork Valley, which trends along the western margin of the park. It is about 10 miles wide, too broad to be an ordinary river valley. Its width, and its remarkable straight north-to-south course, suggest that it must reflect bedrock structure. It seems reasonably clear that the North Fork Valley is a gap in the overthrust slab. The Whitefish Ranger, west of the valley, contains Precambrian sedimentary formations like those in Glacier Park. In Canada just north of Glacier, Cretaceous formations similar to those exposed in the high plains surface in the floor of the North Fork Valley. We would surely see the same formations in the western part of Glacier Park if the younger glacial sediments did not so completely cover the older rocks there.

The easiest way to explain the presence of Cretaceous rocks in the North Fork Valley is to assume that the overthrust slab broke in two. The fragment to become Glacier Park moved 10 miles farther east than the one that became the Whitefish Range. So the North Fork Valley is a window between the two parts of the overthrust slab. It looks down into the relatively young Cretaceous formations beneath ancient sedimentary rocks that we see in the mountains on either side. Compare the Precambrian rock that slid east on the Lewis overthrust fault to a slab of snow sliding down a roof, and then imagine the slab of snow separating into two large pieces, exposing the roof between them.

Eroding the Modern Landscape

Movement on the Lewis overthrust fault created the major elements of the landscape: the blocks of mountains you might see from the moon, not the individual hills and valleys. Those are the legacy of at least 50 million years of patient erosional sculpture that still continues.

During most of the last 50 million or more years, the region had a desert climate, and erosion created landscapes much like those we see in the Southwest deserts today. Then, during the last 2 to 3 million years, a series of great ice ages brought enormous glaciers that carved most of the details of the modern landscape.

Grinnell Glacier. GLACIER NPS

The Desert Years

By the end of the extremely dry climate that persisted for 50 million years, streams had dissected the mountains of Glacier Park into a maze of deep and closely spaced canyons, depositing the debris of their erosion in a blanket of gravel spread far to the east. Although little, if anything, of the old desert landscape survives in the mountains, we can still see large remnants of it on the high plains east of the mountains.

Erosion in dry regions tends to produce expanses of smoothly graded plains underlain by layers of gravel laid down during occasional flash floods. Such plains did exist east of Glacier Park, all the way to the Dakotas. The climate became wetter when the ice ages began, sometime between 2 and 3 million years ago, and modern streams have since carved their valleys into the old desert plains surface. To find bits of the old desert, look for their flat skyline profiles in the uplands between streams east of the mountain front.

The Ice Ages

Between 2 and 3 million years ago, the Earth's climate changed, and great ice ages have come and gone ever since. No one knows what causes the great ice ages, or what ends them. Neither does anyone know how many ice ages there were, when they happened, or how long they lasted. Nor do we know when the next ice age will start, or what may herald its coming.

What we do know is that the glaciers that covered most of Glacier Park during the last ice age nearly obliterated the record of their predecessors, leaving a landscape that could as well have been created during a single ice age as during several. Almost everything we see here in the modern landscape emerged in essentially its present form as the glaciers of the last ice age melted about 10,000 years ago.

Grinnell Glacier viewed from above. CHUCK HANEY

During the height of the last ice age, glaciers as much as several thousand feet thick filled all the valleys in the park. Adjacent glaciers coalesced in many places to spread a nearly continuous ice cap over much of the high country. Many of the mountain glaciers in the western part of the park flowed into the North Fork Valley, ponding there to make a slow-moving sheet of ice 10 miles across.

East of the park, glaciers pouring out of the mountains ponded on the high plains to make a broad expanse of nearly stagnant ice, a "piedmont glacier" along the mountain front. Somewhere between Glacier Park and Browning, that piedmont glacier met and coalesced with the continental glacier spreading southwestward from central Canada. The seam is not obvious in the landscape, but we can determine just where the two glaciers joined by finding the line where glacially transported rocks from the Rocky Mountains meet the entirely different rocks carried in from northern Manitoba.

Glaciers

If more snow falls every winter than can melt the next summer, leftover snow accumulates from year to year and slowly turns into solid ice. As the ice reaches a depth of about 150 feet, it begins to flow plastically as though it were extremely stiff modeling clay. When that happens, the path of ice becomes a glacier. Some glaciers are hardly more than oversized snow patches, but those that carved the landscape of Glacier Park were real ice age monsters, rivers of ice miles long and as much as several thousand feet deep in places.

As far as anyone knows, glaciers that form on mountains never create new valleys. Instead, they invariably pour ponderously down stream valleys that already existed, changing them into glaciated stream valleys. Glaciers erode their valleys in some places, and deposit the eroded sediments in others. The final result, after the ice melts, is a distinctive landscape that tells of glaciation in nearly every detail.

As a glacier moves down its valley, it descends into warmer climates, eventually reaching a level where the ice melts as fast as it advances. That balances stabilizes the front of the ice until the climate changes. An increase in snowfall at high elevation will push the snout of the glacier to lower elevations, where the climate

Lake McDonald in winter. KEVIN LEAGUE

is warm enough to match the increased ice flow. Conversely, decreased snowfall at high elevations will reduce ice flow, causing the snout of the glacier to melt back to a high, and cooler, elevation. As we might expect, glaciers respond to a warming climate by melting back to higher elevations, to a cooling climate by advancing to lower elevations.

The Sandpaper Effect

Glaciers carry enormous quantities of mud, sand, and gravel embedded in the ice, especially in the lower part of the glacier. All that sediment makes the sole of the glacier rasp across bedrock surfaces as though it were a giant sheet of sandpaper. After the glacier melts, the rasped bedrock is left smoothed and covered with parallel grooves called striations. Look almost anywhere in the park for such crudely sandpapered bedrock. The striations record the exact direction of ice movement. On a larger scale, the smoothed bedrock preserves of record of where the ice flowed, and where other processes of erosion shaped the bedrock. That record still survives in some areas of Glacier park 10,000 years after the great glaciers melted.

Look high up the cliffs almost anywhere in the park to see that their lower parts are relatively smooth and their upper parts extremely rough. The smooth and rough areas meet along a sharp line that slopes gently down the valley. That line marks the ice level against the cliff during the height of the last ice age. Sediment embedded in the glacier rasped the lower part of the cliff smooth, while freezing and thawing pried blocks out of the rock above the ice, leaving that part of the cliff ragged. The old ice level is especially easy to see on the cliffs high above Logan Pass and Two Medicine Lake.

In areas where the old ice level is well preserved, it is possible to trace it with the eye from one mountainside to another to mentally reconstruct the glaciers that existed during the last ice age. By doing that, we can see that ice completely filled many a valley and spilled over a divide to coalesce with a glacier in the next valley. Many large areas of the park must have lain beneath an almost continuous ice cap. In much of Glacier Park, only the higher peaks rose above the expanse of ice.

Giant Quarrying Machines

Glaciers erode bedrock mostly by freezing fast to blocks of rock already broken along ancient fractures and then pulling them loose, a process called "plucking." Glacially plucked bedrock surfaces look ragged, as though crudely quarried. Look at almost any of the high cliffs in the park to see examples of glacially plucked surfaces.

The heads of glaciers pluck chunks of bedrock loose more efficiently than any other part. As it moves downslope, the ice draws away from the bedrock behind it, pulling blocks of bedrock loose and opening a gap between rock and ice. Anyone who walks to the head of a glacier must cross that gap to get back onto bedrock, and in many cases that requires quite a jump. Snow and meltwater fill that gap with new ice that freezes fast to the bedrock. Meanwhile, the glacier continues to move down its valley and repeats the process, pulling more chunks of rock loose and opening again the gap between ice and bedrock. Now that the ice has melted, we can see how deeply the heads of the ice age glaciers quarried the mountaintops.

Every glacial valley heads in a large hollow called a cirque, perhaps the most characteristic element of glaciated mountain landscapes. There are hundreds of cirques in Glacier Park. Nearly every peak drops away into cirques on at least one side, most on several sides. In many places, adjacent cirques blend into each other, making it hard to see them individually. In other places, cirques stand alone, looking as though a giant had gouged the mountain with an oversized ice cream scoop. Sparkling little lakes nestle in the floors of many cirques, reflecting the cliffs of the headwall rising to the peak above. Hidden Lake, Avalanche Lake, and Iceberg Lake all are good examples of cirque lakes familiar to many park visitors.

Where several glaciers flowed down a mountain, gouging cirques into the summit from several directions, we now see the jagged remnant of the original peak. It forms a ragged pinnacle that drops away in steep cliffs into the deep cirques below. We call those rocky spires "horn" peaks, an alpine term familiar in the names of such famous mountains as the Matterhorn. Most of the high peaks in Glacier Park are horns.

Gouged Valleys

Every summer, people take thousands of photographs to preserve views of distant peaks reflected in the waters of Lake McDonald or St. Mary Lake. Those really are remarkable scenes, and they could not exist if the great ice age glaciers had not gouged the valleys straight so we could look along them at the distant mountains.

Glaciers are less flexible than rivers and cannot flow so easily around bends in the valleys. So they removed the bends from the original river valleys as though they were bulldozers going down a narrow mountain trail. That also leaves the valley considerably wider than it was before glaciation. And it changes the cross-sectional profile.

Snow dusts the Garden Wall. JOHN LAMBING

Large glaciers tend to gouge their valleys into deeply rounded troughs almost semicircular in crosssection. We see that best in the higher parts of glaciated valleys where very little sediment fills the floor. The bedrock floors of those high valleys typically contain small lakes or ponds called tarns. You can tell that tarns fill a bedrock basin by going to the outlet stream and watching it spill over solid rock.

Glaciers gnaw the ridges separating adjacent valleys into thin rock walls with ragged crests, generally called aretes, a term imported from the Swiss Alps, where the glaciated landscapes resemble those in Glacier Park. The Garden Wall is a good example of an arete familiar to many park visitors. It is so thin near its crest that in one place there is a hole in it. In the Many Glacier area, people enjoy watching the sun shine for a moment through that window as it sets behind the Garden Wall. Before glaciation, that thin wall of rock was the crest of a broad ridge.

Distant view of Bird Woman Falls. NPS/TIM RAINS

Where active glaciers met, their surfaces join at the same level. Now that the ice has melted and exposed the floors of those glaciated valleys, we can see that small glaciers do not carve as deeply as do large glaciers. Tributary valleys stand well above the main valley, and their streams join the main stream over waterfalls or cascades. An example of this is Bird Woman Falls, seen by most park visitors as they travel along the valley of McDonald Creek.

Glacial Moraines

Melting glacial ice dumps a deposit of indiscriminately mixed mud, sand, gravel, and boulders. That material, which looks in a roadcut like something a bulldozer might have scraped together, is called till. It is easy to recognize even where there is no roadcut because glaciers leave boulders littering the surfaces of most deposits. Geologists call any deposit of till a moraine.

There are several kinds of moraines that differ in origin corresponding to the part of the glacier that deposited them. They also differ in appearance. Let's start with the most distinctive kind.

Glaciers deposit a ridge of till around their lower margins where the glacial conveyor belt ends. The result is a terminal moraine that faithfully records the outline of the lower part of the glacier that built it. We don't see many good examples of terminal moraines in Glacier Park because so many of the valley glaciers emptied into either the big piedmont ice sheet along the eastern margin of the park or into the huge glacier that filled the North Fork Valley. However, there are a few small terminal moraines at high elevations that likely formed since the last ice age ended.

Glaciers also deposit till along their sides to build lateral moraines, which make high benches along the valley walls. Lateral moraines are especially prominent on south-facing valley walls at low elevations because more ice

A lateral moraine. GLACIER NPS

melts in those places and therefore deposits more till. Large lateral moraines exist along the lower parts of most of the valleys in the park, and in some places they are very prominent indeed. The ridges on both sides of Lake McDonald, for example, are large lateral moraines, perhaps the most spectacular in the park. And the densely wooded hills along the south side of St. Mary Lake are also large lateral moraines.

Finally, melting glaciers plaster much of the ground beneath them with till to create a rather characterless deposit called a ground moraine. Most of the large valleys in the park have ground moraine here and there in their floors, but we rarely notice them except as expanses of gently undulating terrain full of small ponds and marshes. Glacier till is generally fairly impermeable to water, and ground moraine is especially so because it was compacted beneath the weight of the glacier.

Glacial Outwash

We think of ice ages as cold times, and the climate probably was significantly colder and much wetter than what we know today. But there is no reason to doubt that ice age summers were warm, quite possibly as warm as the summers we know. Summer days were long then, too, and many must have been sunny. Many of us are, after all, descended from people who camped out in the northern climes during the last ice age, and our ancestors seem to have managed quite well.

We know summers were well above freezing because we can see the results, that vast quantities of ice melted off the lower parts of the ice age glaciers every summer, shedding torrents of muddy water into streams. The swollen and muddy streams dropped part of their sediment load to form deposits that geologists call outwash. We can look at the streams that drain from glaciers in Alaska and Canada today and imagine what ours must have been like then: many small and constantly shifting channels braiding their way through a maze of islands. But the muddiest season came as the glaciers melted at the end of the ice age.

Everything we see suggests that the last ice age ended abruptly. At the height of the last ice age, about 11,000 or 12,000 years ago, so much water was tied up in the great glaciers that sea level stood some 300 feet lower than it now does. Then the climate changed, and, within 2,500 years, sea level had risen to its present stand, which means that the ice on land had melted back to about what we see today. Even though we don't know how or why the climate changed, we can easily imagine what the land to be Glacier Park was like during those 2,500 years.

The place was, quite simply, a mess.

When glaciers melt rapidly, they shed torrents of incredibly muddy water and leave behind dreary expanses of mud and gravel. In Glacier Park, all that debris lies just as the melting glaciers left it about 10,000 years ago. Nothing has changed except that trees have since grown, and they improve the view. Consider Lake McDonald and St. Mary Lake, both relics of the last years of the ice age.

Lake McDonald formed as the glaciers melted. Evidently, a large mass of ice was left behind as the glacier rapidly

A grizzly wanders near Sperry Glacier. GLACIER NPS

melted back, and muddy water washed sediment in around it, perhaps partially burying it. When that marooned lump of ice finally melted some hundreds or perhaps thousands of years later, it left the basin that the lake now fills. St. Mary Lake formed at the same time, although in a different way. Glacial meltwater washing into the valley from tributary canyons on both sides deposited large fans of gravel that now impound the lake. The park entrance and visitor center at the lower end of St. Mary Lake stand on that gravel deposit. Similar situations exist in the lower parts of most of the park's large valleys.

Visitors on Sperry Glacier in the early twentieth century.
ARCHIVES AND SPECIAL COLLECTIONS, MANSFIELD LIBRARY, UNIVERSITY OF MONTANA

After the Ice Age

Now that the great ice age glaciers are gone, at least for the time being, other processes of erosion are slowly changing the mountains of Glacier Park. Nevertheless, most of what we see is still left from the last ice age, not the product of modern erosion.

Now streams flow along the valley floors that were filled to the brim with ice a little more than 10,000 years ago. That water is slowly shaping the valley floors into the forms that streams create, but they have not made much progress. The waterfalls and cascades are all remnants of glacial erosion and will all disappear as the streams continue their own work.

The big lakes trap most of the sediment that the modern streams carry, and every particle of mud or sand brings the lake closer to its end. Before too many thousands of years have passed, all the lakes will have filled with sediment and become level plains. In the geologic sense of time, all lakes are temporary and doomed to quick disappearance.

Meanwhile, the tediously slow processes of weather are beginning to break the bare rock into soil, and thus to soften the harsh outlines of the glaciated mountains. But that is an extremely slow process, and we can only wonder how far it may progress before another ice age intervenes. To see how slowly weathering proceeds, look at the glacially striated bedrock almost anywhere in the park and remember that it has probably been ice free and exposed to the elements for about 10,000 years. It is impossible to ponder the freshness of those surfaces without reflecting that soil is not a renewable resource within any humanly meaningful time span, and that soil erosion really is an irreparable loss.

Finally, the modern glaciers: compared to their predecessors of the last ice age, they are nothing. And they have diminished greatly in both size and number since they were first mapped just after the turn of the 20th century. Such small—perhaps miniscule is the better word—glaciers could not by any stretch of the imagination carve the magnificent landscape we see in Glacier Park. Furthermore, the little glaciers we see today appear to be new glaciers that formed sometime after the last ice age, not the shrunken remnants of the ice age giants. The modern glaciers have carved small cirques around the edges of some of the big cirques left from the last ice age, and they have made a few moraines high in the mountains. Otherwise, they have contributed very little to the landscape of Glacier Park.

But who knows? Someday, those little glaciers we see in the highest and shadiest valleys of the park—if they endure our warming world—may grow into the next generation of giants when the next ice age begins.

Belton Bridge, built over the Middle Fork of the Flathead River and now closed to vehicles, was once the main entrance to Glacier National Park. KEVIN LEAGUE

HISTORY

Sinopah Mountain mirrored on Two Medicine Lake. JOHN LAMBING

Peopling the Park

by C.W. Buchholtz

Glacier's rocky peaks, deep-blue lakes, and dense forests have long beckoned to people. Animal trails must have lured early Native American hunters. And we know its cliffs and echoes made enough magic to stimulate legends. The fur trade brought a handful of trappers and traders cautiously venturing through. Mountain passes caught the eyes of railroad engineers, and lucky-looking rocks kept prospectors prowling. Land drew pioneers. Scenic land brought tourists. The abuse of land made conservationists decide to protect this region, and simple aesthetics made others wish to preserve it for future generations. Solitude and natural beauty attracted people looking for rest and recreation.

The wilderness itself reminds us of the past, the way things used to look. It offers a stark contrast to everyday scenes crowded with cars and concrete. It makes us wonder about all those earlier travelers who heard the mountains' call. Even an outline of their visits may help us appreciate what little wild country remains, still preserved for our pleasure.

Tribes and Trails

Exactly who first traveled the trails of today's Glacier Park remains a mystery, despite extensive archaeological exploration here in recent years. Someday, archaeologists may find an ancient campsite, a cache of tools, or some other clues to provide us with a clearer prehistoric picture. Meanwhile we can only speculate about ancient hunters who haunted these mountains. Chances are good that prehistoric hunters roamed through this region thousands of years ago, but evidence of their activity is scant. A few circles of rocks marking old tipi rings still may be spotted along the eastern foothills. An old buffalo skull once was found atop Chief Mountain. But stones and bones merely hint at early people's pursuits of spiritual beliefs.

Our first documented glimpse of the region was provided by Hudson's Bay Company agent Peter Fidler. He was traveling with a Piegan band of Blackfeet, southwestward across the Canadian prairies in 1792. A map Fidler later produced displayed a rough sketch of the Rockies and the name of "Kings Mountain" attached to one of those peaks. Later changed to "Chief Mountain," that prominent landmark of the front range became the first of Glacier's features to gain recognition. What Peter Fidler also discovered, as did a few other traders who probed this area, was the fact that powerful bands of Blackfeet (Blackfoot in Canada) dominated the entire upper Missouri River region and the headwaters of the Saskatchewan River as well.

At that time, the Blackfeet Confederation consisted of the Siksika (Northern Blackfeet), the Kainah (Bloods), and the Piegan (Pikuni). Allied with them were the Gros Ventre (or Big Belly). These warlike bands had extended their power throughout the plains during the 1700s, just after they obtained horses and guns. Their reputation as fearsome warriors spread quickly. Their dominion included vast herds of bison, now theirs to hunt. With plentiful food and hides for clothing, shelter, and equipment, the Blackfeet clearly were masters of Montana's northern plains by the 1790s. For them, Glacier's Rockies acted as a massive western boundary. On occasion, small parties of Blackfeet ventured across the mountains to raid the tribes of the western valleys. Glacier's high passes served those parties well. Very rarely did the Blackfeet bother to hunt mountain animals, however, since their horses and lifestyle were more suited to the prairie.

More accustomed to the mountains were several tribes far less powerful than the Blackfeet. The Kutenai, the Kalispel (or Pend d'Oreille), and the Flathead ranged throughout the forested valleys of western Montana. Until the Blackfeet forced them off the plains, these tribes also had lived and hunted on the prairie. In making the mountains their home, they adopted deer and elk, fish and fowl, and berries and camas roots as their staples—substitutes for the favored buffalo. Once or twice a year, hunting parties from these western tribes bravely ventured east across the mountains, entering the plains to hunt buffalo despite the risk of a Blackfeet attack. One rare tale of such a clash placed the event near Glacier's Cut Bank Creek. There Siyeh (Mad Wolf) and his band of Blackfeet warriors fought some Kutenai who were attempting to return westward across Cut Bank Pass. The Blackfeet, according to the tale, slaughtered and scalped all the Kutenai except for one old woman.

Violence and hostility kept the western tribes confined to the mountains and the Flathead Valley. But their lifestyles adjusted quickly. The Kutenai, in particular, developed a reputation for being skilled hunters of bighorn sheep. Observers marveled at the Kutenais ability to run up steep slopes, and early explorers noted that their leg muscles were large and well-muscled from climbing across ridges.

Another smaller band of natives also frequented the region. Called the Mountain Assiniboine (or Stonies), this group subsisted along the eastern foothills. Forced by the Blackfeet to accept less desirable hunting grounds, the Stonies gained their name from their method of cooking food with heated rocks. The Stonies were few in number and always alert to the movements of their more aggressive neighbors. Deer and elk served as their food supply, with smaller animals like porcupine and grouse adding to their diet. They also ate berries, seeds, and root bulbs, and chewed tree bark in particularly lean times.

Years of hunting and warfare sparked numerous legends and tales. Writers like George Bird Grinnell in the 1880s and James Willard Schultz in the 1920s recorded many Indian stories, some associated with Glacier's mountains. Grinnell's stories of Napi (Old Man) and the Blackfeet genesis are particularly poignant. In part because of Grinnell's and Schultz's writings, a pantheon of tribal chiefs' and heroes' names became attached to Glacier's landscape. Dotting the map are sites named Red Eagle, Curly Bear, Heavy Runner, and Mad Wolf, all recalling famous tribal leaders. Medicine Grizzly, Beaver Medicine, and Windmaker evoke the stuff of legends. A few such names predated Grinnell and Schultz, with Two Medicine Valley obtaining its name from two ceremonial Blackfeet lodges that once graced the area. St. Mary Lakes were called The Lakes Inside before white men arrived.

Through much of the nineteenth century, Blackfeet power kept visitors or invaders away from this territory. Not until constant war, recurrent smallpox epidemics, and whiskey reduced their numbers and will to fight did the Blackfeet weaken their grip on this land. Gradually, trappers and trading posts became more common. Disappearing buffalo herds spelled the end of the prosperity of food and materials, and, tragically, starvation was common among the Blackfeet by the 1880s. At the same time, prospectors were demanding that the Blackfeet relinquish their mountain land. In 1895, the Blackfeet sold the "Ceded Strip" (Glacier's eastern side) for $1.5 million. Decades earlier, western-slope tribes had relinquished all claims to these mountains. Still, today's Blackfeet Reservation, adjacent to Glacier's eastern boundary, reminds us of earlier—and continued—Native American stewardship over the region.

Trappers and Travelers

The Blackfeet's reputation kept most mountain men away from Glacier. Only a handful of trappers or traders left any account of their journeys across these mountains. In 1810, to give one rare example, trapper Finian MacDonald and 150 Indian allies crossed through Marias Pass headed toward the plains. Almost immediately they encountered 170 "Peeagans." The ensuing battle left seven Blackfeet dead and taught men like MacDonald to choose safer routes far to the north or south. Other fur traders simply skirted the region. And only sketchy evidence links the search for beaver pelts with Glacier's waterways. Both Lake McDonald and tiny Rubideau Creek may derive their names from such adventurers.

Blackfeet man and woman in native dress.
ARCHIVES AND SPECIAL COLLECTIONS, MANSFIELD LIBRARY, UNIVERSITY OF MONTANA

Missionaries and map makers also traveled through quickly. Exactly which "Black Robe" paused to christen St. Mary Lake remains a question, but maps soon would display that appellation. In the early 1850s "official" explorers began arriving. Engineer A. W. Tinkham, associated with the Isaac I. Stevens survey, traveled across Glacier in 1853 as he searched for potential railroad routes. He crossed Cut Bank Pass and noted that any railroad built there would require a huge tunnel. In the following year, Stevens dispatched John Doty, who more carefully surveyed all of Glacier's eastern slope. But Doty concluded that none of the mountain passes he observed was suitable for a railroad, leaving Marias Pass to be "rediscovered" in 1889 by another engineer, John F. Stevens.

Heavy Runner Mountain, named for a Blackfeet leader. JOHN LAMBING

Other government surveyors arrived by 1860, this time marking the 45th parallel as the international boundary. With them came artist James Madison Alden, who produced the first scenic watercolors of Glacier's northern mountains. By the 1860s and 1870s, a few prospectors wandered along the western slope. In one sketchy (albeit surprising) report, a 30-ounce gold nugget supposedly was found at Quartz Lake. Those decades also introduced a few itinerant whiskey traders, distributing their products among the Indians along the eastern slope. One such "whiskey fort" established by John Kennedy is remembered only by the name of today's Kennedy Creek.

Additional government surveys in 1874 brought Lt. John Van Orsdale, dispatched from Fort Shaw to observe this area. After visiting Lake McDonald (which he called Lake Terry after his commanding officer), traveling up Nyack Creek, and crossing Cut Bank Pass, Van Orsdale was sufficiently impressed by the country to write a letter suggesting that the region be made a national park. With Yellowstone Park founded only two years earlier, Van Orsdale believed he had spotted another national treasure. But more than two decades would pass before others found merit in his suggestion.

The 1880s ushered in the man who would ensure that the national park idea would succeed. As an authority on Indians and editor of *Forest and Stream* magazine, George Bird Grinnell was influential as well as politically knowledgeable. He originally came to the region to draw public attention to the starving and destitute condition of the Blackfeet. But big-game hunting drew him toward the mountains, and he returned to explore for many years. He also wrote of his experiences in fourteen essays for *Forest and Stream.* Grinnell concluded that "the scenery is grand, game plenty, the fishing unexcelled," and offered the nation the first real publicity about Glacier's mountains. Soon, other men of wealth journeyed here to hunt, with the Baring family of English bankers, Ralph Pulitzer, and Henry L. Stimson typifying adventurers of that era. Geographical names in Glacier, including Singleshot, Fusillade, Gunsight, and Baring, are a few mementos left by those hunters.

Chief Two Guns White Calf, a Blackfeet leader thought to be one of the models for the buffalo nickel, meeting Mike Gibbons.
LIBRARY OF CONGRESS

Native American women play the stick game in Glacier National Park in the first half of the 20th century.
LIBRARY OF CONGRESS

Prospectors also explored this region, with "Dutch Lui" Myers being among the first to find a vein of what he described as "grayish white quartz carrying gold, silver, copper, and some lead" in 1889. But getting the mountains opened to legal prospecting took another nine years. Meanwhile, James J. Hill's Great Northern Railway was snaking its way westward. Once surveyor John F. Stevens declared Marias Pass usable, construction proceeded up Summit Creek and across the Continental Divide, then descended along Bear Creek eventually to parallel the Middle Fork of the Flathead River. Almost overnight, civilization sprouted along the route of the Great Northern Railway, which began service in 1891. Travelers came in greater numbers, with a few taking the time to wander to spots like Lake McDonald. One of those tourists was Dr. Lyman Sperry. A college professor and traveling lecturer, Dr. Sperry was on the lookout for scenic attractions, hoping to add subjects to his lecture list and helping the Great Northern publicize its new route. What enchanted Sperry most was alpine scenery. His interest in glaciers led him to declare that "a man can find anything he wants in this region."

Blackfeet Indians at Trick Falls, about 1917. MONTANA HISTORICAL SOCIETY

Crusaders of Commerce and Conservation

The coming of the railroad introduced a handful of settlers to the western valleys. People like Milo Apgar, Charlie Howes, George Snyder, and a few others carved homesteads out of the forested shoreline of Lake McDonald. Other hardy pioneers drifted to likely spots farther north, especially where meadows offered natural fields. Valleys adjacent to the North Fork of the Flathead River soon boasted a few ranches. The settlers around Lake McDonald quickly realized that scenery was one of their most profitable resources. They began to cater to railway travelers, providing meals, lodging, and boat rides up the lake. A few acted as guides. An infant "Glacier Hotel" soon appeared at the upper end of the lake near Snyder Creek, later to be expanded and become Lake McDonald Lodge. The tourist business had begun.

Backcountry trails, however, served more than just tourists. Persistent prospectors kept searching for signs of wealth. Some promising veins offered hints of copper. Mineral Creek, far up the McDonald Valley, became the site of early exploration and investment by people like Elizabeth Collins, the "Cattle Queen of Montana."

East Side Tunnel on Going-to-the-Sun Road in West Glacier. LIBRARY OF CONGRESS

The clear water of Kintla Lake. CHUCK HANEY

With the eastern slope opened to prospecting in 1898, a flood of excitement and expectation overwhelmed the region. Dozens of claims were filed, many people believing that their strikes would prove as rich as Butte. The settlement of Saint Mary was born in this boom. To the north, in today's Many Glacier area, the town of Altyn claimed leadership of the Swiftcurrent mining district. Several hundred prospectors pawed at nearby slopes. Exploration shafts were sunk, companies were formed, investment was attracted, and a few mines were developed. But yields proved dismal. The boom went bust. Within a year or two most of the miners had left, although a few diehards held on for another decade or more.

At the same time, however, the discovery of oil to the north in Alberta—and also near Kintla Lake—spurred a bit more excitement. A primitive road was carved from Lake McDonald through the forests to the Kintla region, with exploration rigs soon to follow. Small deposits of gas and oil also were discovered in the valleys of the eastern slope. But like the dreams of copper and gold, oil proved to be insufficient to sustain investment. Interest in mining and drilling waned, and by 1907 it was clear that mineral wealth could not be found.

In addition to railroaders, homesteaders, and prospectors, some people with a less exploitive outlook also discovered these mountains. Along with writers and publicists like Grinnell and Sperry came others intending to protect the region. As part of a national conservation movement, Congress permitted the establishment of forest reserves (later called national forests) in 1891. That same year, the Lewis and Clark Forest Reserve was established, which included Glacier's western slope. (Glacier's eastern slope would be added after 1898.) In terms of actual protection or regulation, little changed until 1900. By then, forest rangers had started patrolling the region. Fred Herrig and Frank Liebig guarded against abuses and waste. They fought forest fires, enforced game laws, watched for timber thieves, looked after tourists, and kept the trails open. It was their intent to provide for the orderly development and use of the region's resources.

At the same time, a few people believed that mere conservation did not provide enough protection for the scenic treasures of this region. Advocates of the national park idea began gaining influence, especially once the search for minerals proved futile. George Bird Grinnell, one of the most influential spokesmen for the park idea, promoted the cause in a 1901 article for *Century Magazine* titled "The Crown of the Continent." He argued that recreational and aesthetic concerns demanded more attention in the form of protection. Men like Grinnell and Sperry helped convince Great Northern Railway officials to support the national park concept for Glacier, a politically important move.

Teepees stand at the entrance of Glacier National Park, circa 1914.
WIKIMEDIA COMMONS/HARRIS & EWING COLLECTION

On December 11, 1907, Montana's Senator Thomas H. Carter introduced a bill to create Glacier National Park. Several years of public debate followed. A few local homesteaders feared the loss of their land. Critics of the Great Northern argued that a park would preclude using any of the mountain passes for a railroad route to compete with Great Northern. Some people believed that timber and other park resources—especially wildlife—should be harvested rather than preserved. Nevertheless, those voices of opposition never shouted in unison. And proponents of the park made a few compromises regarding rights of private landowners, valid mineral claims, and water development projects. Compared with other conservation fights, the move to establish Glacier Park was not very controversial. On May 11, 1910, President William Howard Taft signed the bill creating Glacier National Park.

Builders of a National Playground

Glacier's first superintendent, Major William R. Logan, arrived in August 1910. He faced a virtual wilderness (just then plagued by a dry summer during which forest fires blackened nearly 50,000 acres within the park). Logan began his work that season by appointing a ranger force of six men. He also surveyed the region, formulating ideas about developing Glacier into a "playground" more acceptable to modern tourists. Working with other national park planners, Logan later proposed building an extensive grid of roadways, a plethora of hotels, and a vast network of trails. Of all his ideas, the "Transmountain Road" concept proved most popular, later to become Going-to-the-Sun Road.

But the plans of Superintendent Logan and his successors paled in comparison to the immediate investment and construction initiated by Great Northern Railway. Between 1910 and 1917, Great Northern spent $1.5 million developing tourist facilities in Glacier. Nine rustic chalets were constructed at various

backcountry locations (with today's Granite Park and Sperry Chalets still remaining); three tent camps offered more primitive shelters; and a "Mammoth Mountain" hotel was built at Many Glacier, costing a half million dollars. Belton Chalet (at West Glacier) and Glacier Park Lodge (at Midvale, now East Glacier) rested just outside the park near the railroad's depots. A network of roads and trails was built to link these various accommodations.

Over the next two decades, people who visited Glacier followed patterns established by the Great Northern and its hotel company. A majority of tourists arrived by train, disembarking near the large hotel at East Glacier. Riding horses through the park became the primary mode of travel. From East Glacier, trail riders rode to Two Medicine Chalet. From there they headed to Cut Bank Chalet and on to Saint Mary Chalet and Going-to-the-Sun Chalet, crossing the Continental Divide and reboarding the train at West Glacier. Lake launches and auto-bus trips offered optional means of approaching scenic areas. The railroad literature encouraged people to hike as well. At least a week was required to see the park in the manner prescribed for the typical tourist, with some people taking a month or more to "do" Glacier.

That genteel style of tourism became outdated with the building of the Transmountain Road. Once the National Park Service was established, in 1916, funds for such major development projects became available. Surveys conducted in 1917 and 1918 settled the new route across the Continental Divide through Logan Pass. Actual construction took more than a decade and cost some $3 million. On July 15, 1933, Going-to-the-Sun Road officially opened. It was a highway intended for "the great mass of people," cutting through the heart of the park, and meant to introduce visitors to Glacier's wilderness.

Top left: *Many Glacier Hotel from the opposite side of Swiftcurrent Lake, circa 1921.* LIBRARY OF CONGRESS

Center left: *An open-air bus prepares park visitors for a tour.* LIBRARY OF CONGRESS

Bottom left: *Three men standing up in convertible demonstrate the challenge of traveling the park by car.* GLACIER NATIONAL PARK ARCHIVES

Then: *The triple arches on Going-to-the-Sun Road have long helped visitors traverse Pollock Mountain.*
LIBRARY OF CONGRESS

Whether that roadway beckoned people into the backcountry could be questioned. Going-to-the-Sun Road certainly altered the way tourists explored the park. Instead of spending a week or a month winding and wandering along backcountry trails, they could view the "heart" of Glacier in a day. Instead of depending on chalets or tipi camps for food and shelter, they favored campgrounds and motels. In the years to come, an estimated 95 percent of Glacier's visitors confined their visits to that narrow ribbon of roadway. Statistics proved that building the road was a popular idea: only 40,000 people toured the park in 1925, but 210,000 people traveled through in 1936. With this influx of people and automobiles, more facilities were added to provide for the new style of vacationing, with campgrounds and picnic areas (and visitor centers by the 1960s) making the scenic roadway more like a corridor of civilization. Meanwhile, the old and disused chalets and tent camps were destroyed or removed. The tempo of a Glacier Park visit grew faster, and accommodations were designed for more people and shorter stays. By the late 1960s, one estimate showed the average visitor remained in the Glacier area for a mere twenty-five hours.

But during the 1960s a preservationist philosophy began to challenge the value of roadways and rapid visits. An awakened interest in and concern for the environment led more people to forsake their cars to investigate Glacier's backcountry. More hikers meant more sophisticated management techniques, and restrictions were imposed to preserve wilderness values. Adding to that mood, the Wilderness Act of 1964 mandated that vast natural areas within Glacier and other national parks be protected from any further encroachments by civilization.

People demanding environmental quality asked probing questions about the preservation of Glacier's unique features. Concern over the purity of the park's air meant monitoring neighboring industries. Realizing the park's water could be polluted led to refurbishing sanitary facilities. Studies of eagles and elk, grizzlies and ground squirrels, natural fires, and a host of other ecological concerns helped highlight that Glacier, in 1974, was unique enough to be named a World Biosphere Reserve. People slowly rediscovered the fact that Glacier Park was more than just a rapidly passing scene on a cross-country tour. It was a place to be pondered, a place to be preserved and enjoyed.

The call of the mountains changed through the years. The roar of the wind and waterfalls, the whisper of pine, and the echoing call of loons gradually mixed with the hoofbeats of Indian ponies and the muffled tread of Indian trackers. The voices of trappers and traders, explorers and exploiters soon mingled with the curses of miners and the laughter of tourists. The mountains called with an almost mystical allure. At times these Rockies offered passage to the plains, beckoned with the temptation of wealth, and stirred the spirit of adventure. In Glacier National Park, the call of the mountains still can be heard.

Now: *Triple arches continues to support Going-to-the-Sun Road.* CHUCK HANEY

2 New York Tribune October 12, 1919

Courtesy of Mr. L. W. Hill, President Great Northern Railway

Number Eleven of the

Tribune Series *of the* Greatest Scenic Wonders *of* America

Glacier National Park, Mount Jackson

GIGANTIC glaciers of the long ago, descending from the Divide, sculptured these wonderful Montana Rockies of Glacier National Park. From these glaciers mighty cataracts tumble to feed scores upon scores of lovely green lakes in the mountains. From these lakes sparkling mountain torrents rollick away through majestic forested valleys all abloom with wild flowers. Over all the region the Blackfeet, who were once its owners, have woven a mantle of Indian romance. This region was not visited by white men until 1853. It was made a national park by Act of Congress in 1910.

Excerpt from the New York Tribune, *October 12, 1919.* LIBRARY OF CONGRESS

U.S. NATIONAL PARKS NUMBER

PART VI.
NEW YORK TRIBUNE

The Tribune Graphic

SECTION ONE

SUNDAY
MAY 28, 1916

McDERMOTT FALLS and GRINNELL MOUNTAIN, GLACIER • NATIONAL PARK •

Excerpt from the New York Tribune, *May 28, 1916.* LIBRARY OF CONGRESS

Above: *Classic Glacier National Park red jammer bus tour.* CHUCK HANEY

Below: *The United States-Canada border.* CHUCK HANEY

Above: *A woman operates the switchboard at Many Glacier Hotel, circa 1925.*
LIBRARY OF CONGRESS

The lobby of Glacier Park Lodge features logs 36–42 inches in diameter and 40 feet long.
ACROTERION/WIKIMEDIA COMMONS

Lunch Creek flanked by Lewis monkey flower near Going-to-the-Sun Road. CHUCK HANEY

Ranger's Notebook

by R.C. "Bert" Gildart

> ***"Where can I go now and view nature undisturbed?"***
> **John James Audubon, 1846**

LATE ONE EVENING IN GLACIER'S BELLY RIVER COUNTRY, I watched with a small group of companions as a herd of about twenty elk materialized from the woods and slowly grouped along the stream that ran by our camp. For more than an hour the herd meandered along the bank, stopping here and there to quench their thirst. Now and then a calf would kick up its heels and charge through the water.

Suddenly an old bull lifted his head and flicked his ears back and forth—testing the air and trying to locate sounds inaudible to human ears. Then, gradually, we too heard the noise: a sharp crack from the woods that grew louder and louder as the unidentified object moved closer.

The sound of breaking twigs sent the herd galloping across the stream, churning up water as they trotted across the shallows. Then, just as suddenly as they had materialized, they were gone, disappearing into the rapidly descending gloom of night.

Next morning at the crack of dawn, our curiosity aroused, we ambled down to the bank where our elk had been drinking and found tracks made by what appeared from the sign to have been a small black bear. Nothing really dramatic, but, nevertheless, a reminder that we had seen something special— something that one generally sees only in the wilderness.

My companions and I have had many similar experiences in our years of wandering through Glacier's backcountry. Once it was a cow elk swimming across Lincoln Lake; another time it was a porcupine rubbing its quills along the side of our tent during some wee hour of the morning. The point is that it's still possible to enjoy experiences that John James Audubon was searching for back in 1846. We can have these opportunities primarily because Congress decreed in 1916 that a number of areas would be set aside as "vignettes of our National Heritage." Because of a superb system of trails, Glacier is one park that offers easy access to its wilderness areas. Venture along one of them and invariably you will return with indelible memories to savor for years.

Glacier Trails

With more than 700 miles of trails and a wealth of stunning landscapes, Glacier is known as a hiker's park. From easy interpretive walks to extended backpack trips, there's a trail for every age, ability, and ambition. Given so many roadside trailheads and beckoning destinations, first-time visitors are often bewildered by the sheer number of hiking options.

Rest assured that every trail promises beauty and natural wonders, whether in the form of sunlight glinting off a glacial lake beneath a craggy peak or a tiny beetle feeding within the frilly anthers of a beargrass flower. Start with a short stroll, perhaps on the Trail of the Cedars or Swiftcurrent Nature Trail. Then stretch your legs on

Grinnell Trail. CHUCK HANEY

a longer walk to Avalanche Lake, Hidden Lake Overlook, or St. Mary and Virginia Falls. If you're up for a day-long adventure, set your sights on Snyder Lake, the Highline Trail, Piegan Pass, Grinnell Glacier Viewpoint, Iceberg Lake, or No Name Lake and Dawson Pass (with a bonus boat ride across Two Medicine Lake).

The knack for getting the most out of any hike here is to open all your senses and notice every sound, smell, and sight. Feel the air temperature change as you climb a mountainside or approach a waterfall. Which animals have left their tracks in the trail before you? Listen for the squawk and chatter of a Steller's jay or the clatter of rockfall from a cliff face. Can you smell the ripe huckleberry patch before you find the sweet, purple fruit?

Bring a map. It will help you stay found, and you can learn the names of the surrounding peaks and streams. Also bring binoculars. The park is home to more than 260 species of birds, from little nuthatches and kinglets to bald and golden eagles. Hiking is also a great way to see wildlife big and small, and binoculars provide a close-up view from a safe and respectful distance.

For longer hikes and backpack trips, stop at a visitor center or ranger station for the latest trail information. A permit is required for all overnight stays in the backcountry, and a ranger will explain important safety precautions for traveling in bear country.

Mount Jackson. JOHN LAMBING

WINTER ADVENTURES IN GLACIER

Skiers explore the park in the gear of a bygone era.
GLACIER NATIONAL PARK ARCHIVES

Virgin snow lay all around as we skied down the gentle slope of a winding trail and glided slowly onto the white mantle covering Lake Josephine. Here, my partner, seasonal ranger Fred Reese, and I were reminded of the first commandment for winter travelers in Glacier National Park: "Be thou alert to change."

As we rested atop the snow and ice in the middle of the frozen lake, we noticed that the temperature was rising fast. Every gust of wind now seemed to carry an urgent message—Mother Nature presided here, but she might be fickle!

Half an hour earlier, the cold wind had been intense enough to drive a throbbing pain under our wool hats and into our heads. Now, well past the center of the lake, it was too warm to ski wrapped in our down parkas. Our thermometer hovered near 40 degrees Fahrenheit, a rise of more than 45 degrees in the past two hours.

We hurried to the far shore and began applying a wax for warmer conditions to the bottoms of our skis. As we did, we watched the wind whipping snow across the lake and off the surrounding mountain peaks, snow not yet compacted by the warm sun and wind.

Then Mother Nature growled!

Along the far ridge, a dull roar began and soon filled the air. The mountains seemed to groan from every direction and with such a vehemence that is was difficult to locate the exact source of the sound. Our eyes, however, were not confused, and were drawn to Grinnell Point towering above us. Huge slabs of snow and ice slid down the peak and onto Lake Josephine where we had just traversed. Enormous boulders cascaded down the slope, upending trees and sending plumes of snow into the air. Then just as quickly as it started, all motion ceased, the roar abated, and wind gusts were again audible.

Philosophizing as much to myself as to Fred, I said, "For once, we chose the right path!" Fred nodded and added, "And none too soon."

Winter is an enchanting season in Glacier, but also a hazardous one. Storms bring copious snowfall, scouring hurricane-force winds, and wild temperature fluctuations. Snow loads on steep mountainsides turn much of the park into prime avalanche terrain. Even expert, experienced winter travelers can get into trouble here. (In fact, the park strongly discourages venturing onto any of the park's frozen lakes as snow can hide thin or unstable ice.) This, and the fact that most park roads are closed and sleeping beneath deep snow, means that few people enter the park, leaving it to the ravens and jays, moose, mountain goats and bighorn sheep, wolves, mountain lions, and supremely winter-adapted wolverines.

Lake McDonald in winter. KEVIN LEAGUE

The most popular cross-country ski trips in the park center on the Lake McDonald area, Polebridge, and the Two Medicine Valley. At Apgar Village, you can ski on the unplowed Inside North Fork Road and trails to McGee Meadows, returning on the unplowed Camas Road for an 11.5-mile loop. When snow conditions aren't too icy, some people enjoy skiing up the trail to Apgar Lookout, a 10.5-mile out-and-back best suited to those experienced on steeper terrain.

Farther up the lake's east shore on the Going-to-the-Sun Road, skiers can park at the gate at Avalanche Creek and ski up the unplowed road 1.8 miles to a bridge over McDonald Creek with a view upstream to McDonald Falls. From here, turn right at the west end of the bridge and ski another mile along the west bank of the creek to Sacred Dancing Cascade where a footbridge carries you back across the creek to the road and your return route to your vehicle. Another option here is to ski 2.3 miles up to Avalanche Lake. Ask beforehand about conditions—the route may be extremely icy, making the climb strenuous and the downhill return treacherous, and large avalanches off Mount Cannon have occasionally approached the Avalanche Lake Trail.

Death camas.
BERT GILDART

At Polebridge, a 4-mile, mostly level out-and-back to Big Prairie offers views of the North Fork of the Flathead River and the Whitefish and Livingston Ranges. For a longer outing, ski the unplowed road to the foot of Bowman Lake, a 12-mile out-and-back.

The unplowed Two Medicine entrance road offers easy skiing through a beautiful landscape. It's 6 miles round-trip to the park boundary and 10 miles round-trip to Running Eagle Falls. Again, check conditions beforehand—temperatures often change rapidly on the park's east side, and winds can either create a challenging crust or scour the ground free of snow altogether.

Above: *Swiftcurrent Creek, Wynn Mountain, and Allen Mountain in Many Glacier area—prime bear country.* CHUCK HANEY
Below: *Avalanche Creek Gorge near Trail of the Cedars.* JACOB W. FRANK/GLACIER NPS

Grizzly bears in Glacier can weigh up to 600 pounds. CHUCK HANEY

What About the Bears?

Many people are drawn to Glacier National Park not just for the scenery but by the presence of bears. Both black and grizzly bears inhabit the park, and the probability of seeing a bear is fairly high if you know when and where to look, or if you simply get lucky. Bears are beautiful, intelligent, and endlessly fascinating, but as the largest land carnivores in North America, they are also potentially dangerous. It's a wise visitor who takes the time to learn a little about the life histories and habits of these magnificent apex predators.

From fossil remains, researchers believe that black bears *(Ursus americanus)* first emerged about two to four million years ago. Brown bears *(Ursus arctos)*, known as grizzly bears in North America, came much later, with the earliest fossils yet found dating to about 500,000 years ago. They share a common ancestor, *Ursus minimus,* which was widespread in Europe five million years ago and likely radiated to Asia. As these bear species spread throughout Europe, Asia, and eventually North America, they encountered varied habitats and environmental factors that influenced their evolution and behavior.

Black bears have strong hooked claws that make them expert tree climbers. BRIGITTE WERNER/PIXABAY

Black bears became well adapted to living in forests. Their relatively short, curved claws and smaller body size enabled them to climb trees for food and to escape danger. Changes in the climate and the expansion of bear populations northward as ice sheets retreated gradually favored adaptations to more open landscapes such

Grizzly bear. BERT GILDART

as grasslands and tundra. As a result, Ursus arctos developed longer claws and powerful shoulder muscles for digging to reach underground rodents and the roots, tubers, and bulbs of plants. These muscles form the prominent shoulder hump of the modern grizzly. Today, we think of grizzlies as denizens of a few remote tracts of the Rocky Mountain West, Canada, and Alaska, but we should remember that they once ranged across the plains as far east as western Missouri and Iowa, and south into much of Texas. Today, grizzlies are once again roaming eastward onto the prairies of west-central Montana.

Dr. Stephen Herrero, a professor of animal behavior and ecology and author of Bear Attacks: Their Causes and Avoidance, supports the theory that black bears evolved to respond to threats by climbing trees, while grizzlies, adapted to open ground, had but two options: run from danger or advance assertively toward it. For both species, these characteristic behaviors would be firmly imprinted on the cubs when the mother bear took one action or the other. (Not surprisingly, most grizzly bear attacks today involve mothers with their cubs.) It's important to realize that these generalized behaviors do not always apply to individual bears. Black bears do sometimes respond aggressively toward perceived threats, and grizzlies, despite their reputation, usually try to avoid encounters with people. Nevertheless, it's wise to remember that any bear you meet has its own personality, and its behavior will vary depending on the situation and the bear's demeanor at that moment.

North American populations of Ursus arctos include coastal brown bears, inland grizzlies, and barren ground grizzlies of the high Arctic. The very largest of these are found in southwestern Alaska, on Kodiak Island. Hunters have killed bears there that measured nine feet, two inches from the tips of their noses to the end of their short tails. One taken on Kodiak Island weighed an incredible 1,656 pounds. In Glacier, bears are not nearly this big—the largest top out at about 600 pounds.

Despite their bulk, grizzlies are surprisingly agile. On the straightway, bears are fast and have great endurance. A grizzly in Yellowstone Park, running ahead of an automobile, was clocked at 30 miles an hour; a bear's top speed may be 35 miles per hour or more. Biologists tell us that a grizzly's eyesight is about as good as ours, their hearing is acute, and they can smell a carcass from as far as twenty miles downwind.

Both black and grizzly bears gorge themselves in the fall and attain their greatest weight in October just before their long winter sleep. They dig their winter dens in early fall; grizzlies favoring sites on north-facing slopes at higher elevations. With the onset of the season's first big snowstorm, bears retire to their dens to hibernate.

During winter in the den, a bear's body temperature drops six to eight degrees, and its heart beat and breath rate slow markedly. Despite this, bears can rouse from sleep and sometimes emerge from their dens even in midwinter.

Most bears in Glacier come out of hibernation in April, and they tend to be hungry. In their search for food, bears may be drawn to human sources. Spring is the season when they break into cabins, notably in the North Fork country of Glacier Park.

Bears breed from May to July, and, at such times, the males fight viciously for the chance to mate with a female. When dominance has been established and the lesser bear driven from the area, the female and remaining male become very playful. Courtship lasts for a week or more, and, after mating, the male will wander off to seek another receptive female.

Cubs are born in January or February, while the female is in its winter den. Twins are usual, but triplets are common, and occasionally quadruplets occur. At birth, grizzly cubs are covered with short gray hair, and their eyes and ears are sealed. At birth, a grizzly cub is eight to ten inches long and weighs up to one pound.

Young bear cubs play with gentle bites, slaps, and chasing—but unlike children, they play silently without vocalizing. BERT GILDART

Black bear cubs' play teaches them tricks of survival in Glacier National Park. BERT GILDART

Mother bears are strict disciplinarians. The cub that does not heed its mother's command is given a swat that sends it sprawling. The cubs stay with their mother until they are two years old, which means that most females breed only every third year.

Grizzlies rarely climb trees, but they can and sometimes do so to obtain food or to neutralize a perceived threat. In September 1980, a grizzly climbed high into a tree in pursuit of several hikers near Elizabeth Lake. But the hikers climbed even higher! Denali National Park in Alaska has documented three instances of grizzlies climbing trees and injuring people who sought safety in the branches, and in 2005, a woman jogging near Canmore, Alberta, climbed a tree to escape a four-year-old grizzly only to be pulled down and killed.

This leads us to the million-dollar question: How safe is it to hike and camp in grizzly country? Prior to 1967, there had never been a fatal mauling in Glacier National Park. But on August 13 that year, two young women were killed by grizzlies in the course of a single night, in two different locations separated by about twelve linear miles. That summer, I was a road patrol ranger and shortly after midnight was conducting a routine patrol over Logan Pass. Suddenly I heard on my park radio a voice from Granite Park Chalet, a back-country hostel about eight miles away. To no avail they were trying to reach headquarters, but from my location I could hear the voice clearly and was able to relay the message explaining that a woman had been critically mauled and that medical attention was urgently needed. Assured the message was understood, I returned that night to my apartment in West Glacier about 3 A.M. and tried to sleep. But several hours later, Ranger Norm Hagen woke me and said that I was needed immediately at Trout Lake—that a young woman had been mauled there. I was confused and could not believe that yet another mauling had occurred. Sadly, Norm told me that the nineteen-year-old woman at Granite Park had just died.

Quickly, I drove around Lake McDonald to the trailhead near the Lake McDonald Ranger Station, then rushed along the five-mile trail into Trout Lake, meeting Leonard Landa, the McDonald ranger. He'd been alerted by Trout Lake campers who were fleeing the area, saying the young woman had been dragged from her sleeping bag. Landa had returned with the campers to the area. As I got the story from Landa, a helicopter arrived and the pilot handed us firearms. The three of us fanned out and began a search—hoping for the best. But moments later, Landa called out softly, "Here she is."

We loaded the woman's body onto the helicopter, the pilot departed, and we remained in order to provide an armed escort for the campers as they trekked back to the road. Several days later, the chief ranger dispatched Landa and me back to the Trout Lake area, instructing us to base ourselves out of the Arrow Lake Patrol Cabin and search for bears—and to "Kill any you encounter!"

The next morning, I stepped outside the cabin and there, about 100 feet away, was a humped-back bear watching me. I called for Landa to bring out the rifles, and when the bear started moving toward us, we fired. An autopsy of the bear confirmed we had shot the right one. It also revealed that the bear had glass embedded in its molars and that the bear was an emaciated seventeen-year-old sow weighing less than 300 pounds.

About a week later, the park's chief ranger and I helicoptered back to Trout Lake and filled seven burlap sacks with garbage. The helicopter could not handle any more! Simultaneously, garbage was being removed from the dump near Granite Park Chalet. Garbage was not only flagrant there but was so abundant throughout the park that a national outcry demanded an evaluation of backcountry conditions. And then the nation called for the implementation of a bear management plan, which the park lacked at the time.

That introductory plan was basic and sought to separate people and bears. For starters, regulations prohibited dogs in the backcountry because they can antagonize bears and the resulting skirmishes too often spread to the dogs' owners. The plan also recommended that people not hike alone and that women not hike during their menses (a precaution that was later determined to be unfounded).

The plan evolved and specified that bears frequenting areas of human habitation be tranquilized and then relocated. If they returned, they were to be euthanized. As well, if a bear frequented a campground, signs were posted alerting people to the situation. Strict rules governing food storage were also established and essentially required that food items—including coolers—must be stored in closed vehicles.

Over time, the plan evolved and required backcountry visitors to watch a video summarizing bear country rules. It also offered advice for hikers, particularly for those hiking in dense woods. "Sing songs or just make noise," suggested rangers, but should you encounter a bear, "Don't run." If the bear charged, the recommendation was to try to remain calm and stand tall. David Shea, the park's first officially designated bear biologist, had done exactly that and then "charmed" a bear by talking to it quietly. "Good bear," he has said on several such occasions, "good bear." That's appropriate advice if you can do it, but most of us might be just as well off to fall to the ground, curl into a fetal ball with hands protecting the back of our neck, and play dead. That, too, has proven to deescalate a bear encounter.

Bears and Humans

Immediately after the two 1967 fatalities, many people questioned the value of preserving grizzly bears, but virtually all bear experts countered that an ecosystem without g-bears is incomplete. Glacier was established to provide a wilderness environment for both wildlife and people, and when not compromised, it does just that. Here, you can savor the thrill of watching North America's largest omnivore loping across the face of such towering mountains as Siyeh and Grinnell, swimming across the glacial-blue waters of Swiftcurrent or McDonald Lakes, or flinging hunks of rock and sod to expose a marmot in its den. Significantly, the bear management plan secures these experiences and reflects the progress of historical research and improved management techniques. Records indicate that Glacier's bear population reached a low in 1915, which coincided with the heyday of sheep ranching outside the park. Sheep herders shot virtually any bear they encountered, and park managers encouraged rangers do the same. But that philosophy changed about 1920, when park managers began to acknowledge the importance of predators. No longer were bobcats, wolverines, foxes—and bears—considered to be "bad" animals. Rather, biologists recognized their role in shaping behaviors and populations of other animals, and managers began to include predators in their surveys to ascertain their numbers and preferred habitats. For years, however, that was a guess-and-by-golly procedure.

Today, advances in DNA technology allow biologists to study and monitor bear populations with a bit more precision. By collecting and analyzing bear fur, researchers can identify individual bears; determine their species, sex, and relatedness to other bears; assess genetic diversity; and estimate the population size and density of bears in the greater Glacier region. The initial challenge was how to obtain bear hair without harming the bear (or the researchers), and the answer was ingenious. In 2004, inspired by research methods pioneered in Canada, Dr. Kate Kendall began collecting bear hair noninvasively by placing bits of barbed wire around pungent bait in the backcountry. Over the course of her fifteen-year study 34,000 fur samples were collected in Glacier and in the Bob Marshall Wilderness Complex.

Kendall concluded that the entire study area contained an estimated 765 grizzlies. About 300 of these lived in Glacier, which also held about 500 black bears, for a total average density of about one bear for every eight square miles. This was presumed to be the park's carrying capacity. Though Dr. Kendall retired in 2014, her work continues and has even been carried over to studies on other species such as wolverines.

Researchers can also extract DNA from bear scat, allowing them to identify individual bears. Managers sometimes use this information to confirm, for example, that a particular bear is repeatedly frequenting a campground, which means the bear has become habituated to humans. To remedy this dangerous situation, they can relocate the bear well away from people.

Under the bear management plan, park regulations also help prevent bears from becoming problems in the first place. Visitors must stay a minimum of 100 yards from bears at all times. Campers must keep their site clean and store all food, cookware, and other attractants (such as toothpaste) in a hard-sided vehicle or park-designated food locker. Garbage goes into bearproof trashcans. At most backcountry campsites, the park provides facilities for hanging food and garbage; in some areas, campers may use an approved bear-resistant cannister. Never put garbage into pit toilets. Following these regulations protects you and other visitors, and it also protects the bears. Problem bears—particularly those that return after being relocated—sometimes must be killed, a task that no ranger enjoys. (In 2016, a problem bear that was re-captured in Glacier was spared and moved instead to the Grizzly and Wolf Discovery Center in West Yellowstone, where "Sampson" has since awed visitors.)

Instead of removing bears, one management strategy removes people from the equation. The park sometimes closes specific trails when bears are using an area. Biologists know when and where bears are likely to dig for glacier lily bulbs or dine on huckleberries, so trails into habitats rich with those food sources may be closed at appropriate times. Other areas may be temporarily closed on a case-by-case basis due to recent bear activity. One more strategy focuses on people: issuing a citation to anyone caught feeding bears. Tragically, a fed bear often becomes a dead bear because it has learned to associate people with food. Violators who feed wildlife face stiff fines. DON'T FEED THE ANIMALS!

Since 1967, Glacier has seen additional fatal bear attacks, mostly from accidental g-bear encounters, particularly when a hiker surprises a sow with cubs. But misplaced bravado has also cost lives, most flagrantly in 1987 when a photographer hiking alone aggressively pursued a sow with cubs and got too close. When the sow charged, the man tried to climb a tree, but the bear pulled him down and fatally mauled him.

Not all maulings are fatal—bears sometimes take a few defensive swats or bites and then leave. And we should remember that bears are well down the list of lethal hazards in the park. Far more park visitors meet their demise from other causes—the top four being falling, drowning, heart attacks, and vehicle accidents. (To put all mortality causes in perspective, see the book, *Death & Survival in Glacier National Park,* Farcountry Press, 2017.) In the 107 years between the park's establishment in 1910 to 2017, with millions of people visiting the park in that span, bear maulings account for just ten deaths. Bear management specialist David Shea likes to remind people to enjoy the trails and wildlife, noting that "You are much, much safer hiking in Glacier National Park than you are driving to Glacier National Park."

Take bear spray when hiking in Glacier—and know how to use it!
NEAL HERBERT/NPS

That said, visitors should remember that all of Glacier is bear country. Be alert, travel in groups, and carry bear spray, a pepper-based deterrent, whenever you hike. Bear spray is proven to work, but be sure to read the instructions, carry the spray on your hip (not inside a pack), and perhaps even practice a few "fast draws." Then venture out and into one of the nation's best-preserved natural areas that still contains all components of a truly wild land. With luck you may see a bear near Hidden Lake, on the flanks of Swiftcurrent Mountain, or even while driving in Many Glacier. Here, you might look up to the slopes of Mount Altyn. Study its variegated vastness closely and with perseverance you'll see a bruin moving prodigious amounts of dirt or lumbering across the slope while grazing on grasses. It's impossible not to be awed if the bear then stands to sniff the breeze, revealing all of its seven feet of magnificent height and dazzling silver-tipped fur. Should that happen, you'll most likely agree that, thanks to years of wildlife research, thoughtful policy development, and professional ranger services, the bear management plan is working well.

Hiking in bear country locations like Hidden Lake is safe if you are alert and prepared. KEVIN LEAGUE

Battlement Mountain in the Lewis Range is in an alpine subarctic climate zone. KEVIN LEAGUE

The Natural World

by Bob Frauson

Glacier Park Micro-Climate

Glacier National Park makes its own weather (micro-climate) due to its location straddling the Continental Divide. The predominant weather influence is the flow of moist, warm air from the Pacific, which loses heat as it rises over the west slope of the Continental Divide. Moisture is lost in the lower elevations as rain. Rain turns to snow as the air cools over the mountains. This same cool air then plunges down the eastern slope, gaining speed and warming to become chinook winds.

Cold fronts from the Arctic flow southward along the eastern slopes, forcing their way under the warmer Pacific air. Fronts may be visible as fog or clouds that form at the contact points between air masses, and lightning even may occur from violent frontal clashes. Large Arctic fronts tend to spill over the passes (Logan, Marias, etc.) and flow down into western valleys, filling them with cold air that is trapped under the warm, overriding air flowing east. This warm air plummets down the east slope as chinooks, and can create winds gusting in excess of 100 miles per hour. In such storms, the rotating cups on anemometers sometimes spin so fast that centrifugal force destroys them.

North winds are the result of a constant pressure of chilling air moving south at five to ten miles per hour. Elk herds in winter tend to move into these southbound storms and have been known to move as far as eight miles in one night, leaving the boundaries of the park.

Cloud formations can signal weather changes. Altocirrus clouds (mares' tails) move in from the west, usually preceding fronts. Lenticular (lens shaped) clouds denote high winds from the west. These often coalesce into a single long cloud called a chinook arch that can extend north and south from horizon to horizon. In fall and winter, clouds often shroud the Continental Divide and its peaks for days on end. At other times, hat-like "cap clouds" settle on the major peaks.

It can snow in Glacier Park any month of the year. Sometimes snow briefly closes Logan Pass as early as the second week in July. The park can usually count on a snowstorm on Logan Pass the third or fourth week of August, followed by a beautiful Indian summer. Snow that falls in the western valleys is likely to contain more moisture than east-slope snow. The rate of snowfall is a good indicator of avalanche danger. If it exceeds one inch per hour, winter travelers in mountainous terrain must beware. Whiteouts or ground blizzards can occur at any time, even many days after a snowfall, when there are strong winds and loose snow. Orientation is difficult under these conditions. A friend once described the difficulty of skiing in a whiteout as "like skiing inside a ping-pong ball."

Temperature ranges are extreme and can change rapidly. You may start on an afternoon cross-country ski trip from Hudson Bay Divide to St. Mary (seven-plus miles) in minus 25 F. weather, with beautiful gliding conditions, only to have the temperature rise within hours to 45 F. above with rain. The snow becomes as sticky as mashed potatoes. But temperatures can also stay in the minus 25 F. to minus 35 F. range for a week or so at a time. It sometimes dips to minus 50 F. Goats are good barometers of such weather fluctuations. Note their position on the mountainside: if they are high on the slopes, the weather will be good; when they are low, watch out!

Tornados in Glacier?

As mentioned earlier, Glacier can experience winds of hurricane force or higher, and the locals have long acknowledged this. In a high cirque just below the east face of Swiftcurrent Mountain, for example, lies aptly named Windmaker Lake. The highest wind speed recorded to date in the park occurred in April 2014 when an anemometer on Logan Pass registered a gust at 139 miles per hour.

In the spring of 1963, strong winds converged down the Swiftcurrent and Grinnell Valleys, creating a twister. The swirling winds targeted Many Glacier Hotel, tearing balconies and sections of roof from the old hotel. The tornado also slammed into a large, log garage in the parking lot, scattering logs for about a half mile along the Cracker Lake Trail as far as the Governor's Pond. Power lines were downed in the area, starting small forest fires.

Surprise Floods

One of the worst floods to ever occur in Montana affected nearly 30,000 square miles of the state, including Glacier. Beginning on June 7, 1964, heavy rains drenched the region. The Lake McDonald area saw ten inches of rain in twenty-four hours; some places east of the divide received as much as thirteen inches in the same period. This deluge happened to follow heavy snowfalls in April and May; mountain soils were saturated and could hold no more. Streams and rivers roared out of their banks. Great Falls and Kalispell were flooded, but the Blackfeet reservation suffered the worst losses—265 homes destroyed, 20,000 acres of cropland wiped out, and 30 people killed. In and around Glacier, the rains washed out roads, railroad tracks, and bridges.

Historically, flooding here is most likely in June, but exceptions do occur. In early November 1989, heavy snows in the high country closed the Going-to-the-Sun Road over Logan Pass. A freakish weather pattern then hit the park with heavy rain for several days, melting snow at all elevations. Frost in the ground prevented water absorption, making for a heavy runoff. The North and Middle Forks of the Flathead River jumped to flood stage quickly, inundating lowlands along the park boundaries. Railroad embankments were washed out. The Middle Fork surged to five feet above flood stage. Luckily, cool temperatures soon slowed the melt and the high waters subsided. Nearby Hungry Horse Reservoir on the South Fork of the Flathead River rose eight feet in a short period of time.

A stormy day at Lake McDonald. Combined with spring snow melt, storms with heavy rainfall can cause flooding in Glacier. TIM RAINS/NPS

Above: *Belton Bridge, formerly the main entrance to the park, is now closed to vehicles.*
WIKIMEDIA COMMONS/HISTORIC AMERICAN BUILDING SURVEY

Below: *Old Belton Bridge in West Glacier pictured during the historic flood that hit Montana in 1964.*
GLACIER NATIONAL PARK ARCHIVES

Triple Divide

Of all the mountains in Glacier National Park, Triple Divide Peak plays a unique geographic role. Rising to a modest elevation of 8,005 feet, the peak can be reached by trail from the campground in Cut Bank Valley. An eight-mile hike climbs to Triple Divide Pass. From here, an hour-long scramble marked by rock cairns leads to the summit.

From the pyramidal peak, waters drain eastward down Atlantic Creek, eventually joining the Missouri River to reach the Gulf of Mexico and the Atlantic Ocean. To the west, water flows down Pacific Creek to ultimately mingle with the blue Pacific Ocean at the mouth of the Columbia River. And on the north side of the pass, water drains down Hudson Bay Creek and then via the Saskatchewan and Nelson Rivers to Hudson Bay. Thus it's the only peak in the United States to drain into three oceans—the Atlantic, Pacific, and Arctic. Mount Snow Dome in the Canadian Rockies also claims triple-divide status, with runoff flowing to the Pacific, Arctic, and Atlantic. But this depends on how you interpret Hudson Bay—some authorities place it with the Arctic Ocean, while others tie it to the Atlantic. Regardless, Triple Divide Peak offers an excellent perch from which to ponder a raindrop's three possible journeys to such distant destinations.

View south from Triple Divide Peak.
FROM GLACIER NATIONAL PARK: ITS TRAILS AND TREASURES *BY MATHILDE EDITH HOLTZ AND KATHERINE ISABEL BEMIS*

Wolves

Wolves were once an integral part of the ecosystem in the land that became Glacier National Park. But by the 1930s, aggressive hunting and a park philosophy that promoted the preservation of elk, deer, moose, and other prey species contrived to eliminate predators. Rangers hunted wolves, and trapped, poisoned, and shot other meat eaters such as wolverines, coyotes, and bears. Today, park managers recognize the ecological importance of predators, including wolves.

Except for occasional sightings of isolated wolves, the species was absent from Glacier National Park until the early 1980s, when a female denned in the North Fork area and gave birth to five pups. She was part of what researchers called the Magic Pack, and scientists were able to fit some of the wolves with radio collars to track their movement. It soon became clear that wolves ranged over a large area spanning parts of Alberta, British Columbia, Montana, and northern Idaho. One female wolf radio collared in Alberta in 1991 and nicknamed Pluie (PLOO-ee), covered an area of more than 38,000 square miles in nine months, from north of Banff townsite to southeast of Browning, south of Kalispell, and just north of Spokane, Washington.

Gray wolf howling. BERT GILDART

Biologists say that since their return, wolves are thriving in Glacier, with six to eight packs using territories that include land within the park. They readily roam across boundaries—from the park onto adjacent national forest, tribal, and private lands, and back and forth across the U.S.-Canada border. They've been sighted throughout the park, sometimes near roads and on occasion even within a half mile of a visitor center or campground. Perhaps the best chance of seeing or hearing a wolf is in the North Fork area of the park's northwestern corner and along the Camas Road, particularly at dawn or dusk. Rangers remind visitors to stay at least 100 yards from wolves (and bears) and enjoy them through binoculars or a spotting scope.

Middle Fork of the Flathead River near the confluence with the North Fork. GLACIER NPS

Due to the Continental Divide and the park's extreme range in elevations, from its lowest point at the confluence of the Middle and North Forks of the Flathead River to its highest peak Mount Cleveland, Glacier's ecosystem can be divided into five different animal and plant life zones.

The peak of Mount Cleveland rises high behind Goat Haunt Mountain. GLACIER NPS

Life Zones

by R.C. "Bert" Gildart

Glacier's landscape ranges in elevation from 3,150 feet above sea level at the confluence of the Middle and North Forks of the Flathead River to 10,466 feet atop the park's highest peak, Mount Cleveland. The park also spans the Continental Divide, with a generally warmer, wetter climate on the west side and a cooler, dryer one on the east. These factors combine to create five different life zones of plant communities and certain animals that rely on them. Certainly, any of these living things is interesting in itself, but each becomes even more thought-provoking when you understand how it interacts with its habitat and the other inhabitants of that life zone. Let's consider each life zone and its representative plant and animal species.

Grasslands or Bunchgrass Prairie

Although scattered sites of bunchgrass and its associated vegetation range up to 6,000 feet, the fescue grassland community generally occurs at elevations below 5,000 feet. East of the Continental Divide, you'll find prairie-like areas on lower south-facing slopes and valley bottoms, with stands of cottonwood and other deciduous trees and shrubs. One such prairie area is found between St. Mary and Rising Sun along the Going-to-the-Sun Road. Another occurs along the entrance road to Glacier's sister park, Waterton Lakes National Park, in Alberta. Grassy meadows also occur along the North Fork of the Flathead River along the park's western boundary, including, notably, Big Prairie. Animals of this zone include bison (in Waterton), badger, elk, and coyote.

Elk. HARRY COLLINS PHOTOGRAPHY/SHUTTERSTOCK

Aspen Parkland

Forming a transition belt between the grasslands and the conifer forests above, aspen parklands are found in the valley bottoms on the east side of the park, as well as widespread just beyond the park's boundary. Aspen is the dominant tree, along with black cottonwood. Patches of nutrient-rich fescue and other grasses intermingle with shelterbelts of trees, and this zone provides critical winter range for elk and deer. Muskrat and beaver make homes in the marshes and shrubby wetlands here.

North American beaver. GLACIER NPS

Aspen grove. JOHN LAMBING

Montane Forest

Pine marten. CHUCK HANEY

The lower elevation conifer forests blend with poplars and smaller deciduous trees and shrubs such as Rocky Mountain maple, paper birch, and juniper. Douglas-fir, white spruce, and limber pine are notable trees of this zone, and on the park's west side are groves of western red cedar, western hemlock, western larch, lodgepole pine, and a few scattered ponderosa pines. Along Camas Road and around Apgar, you'll find lodgepole or western larch forest, indicative of frequent and severe wildfires. This is a successional community that, if it doesn't burn, will ultimately lead to spruce-fir or cedar-hemlock forests. Elk and deer frequent this zone, as do black bears, mountain lions, and pine marten.

Western larch needles change color each fall and blaze like golden flames. People unfamiliar with these trees may wonder why the forest is full of dying trees. But larches are one exception to the rule that members of the family Pinaceae retain their leaves or needles. (Another exception is the bald cypress that proliferates in the Florida Everglades.) These larches, then, are properly designated as deciduous conifers; they shed their needles in the fall and stand naked through the winter. But before the needles fall, they turn the most beautiful, deep golden color imaginable. Next spring, the trees will blossom with scarlet female flowers and smaller, delicate yellow male flowers. A few weeks later, the larch shimmer with new light-green needles. Dead larches provide homes for cavity-nesting birds—one old larch was found to house twenty nesting pairs of twelve different avian species.

Mountain lion. MOOSE HENDERSON/SHUTTERSTOCK

Glacier's pocket of western red cedars and western hemlocks represents the easternmost range of these species. They are confined to a relatively small portion of the McDonald Creek drainage between lower Avalanche Creek and the shoreline of upper Lake McDonald. Here, where rain and snow are abundant and the humidity is relatively high, a few trees reach great dimensions, as much as 220 feet tall and 7 feet in diameter. Walk the Trail of the Cedars at Avalanche Creek to learn more about this community. White-tailed deer, moose, and red squirrels feed in these dense, damp forests.

Above: *Moose.* CHUCK HANEY

Left: *Red squirrel enjoys its diet of seeds and cones.* GLACIER NPS

Below: *Whitetail buck.* WILLIAM T. SMITH/SHUTTERSTOCK

Subalpine Zone

This life zone receives heavy snowfall that arrives early and lingers late into spring. That means a short growing season for the trees and other plants that grow here, but at least they are abundantly watered. Spruce and fir trees dominate here, including Engelmann spruce and Douglas-fir at lower elevations grading into subalpine fir and whitebark pine up to treeline. Spruce and true firs (genus *Abies*) tend to prefer wetter, north-facing slopes, while pines and Douglas-fir (genus *Pseudotsuga,* "false hemlock," but more closely related to larches) are more tolerant of drier, south-facing slopes. At treeline, a few trees, stunted by the harsh conditions, eke out a life as krummholz, twisted by the wind and snow, with growth rings densely packed.

The subalpine goes fairly quiet in winter, but many animals frequent the zone during summer and fall, including grizzly and black bears, wolverines, mule deer, Clark's nutcrackers and dusky or blue grouse flock to stands of whitebark pines for the nutritious nuts, as do red squirrels, which cache great piles (middens) of the nuts that are then raided by bears.

Wolverine. BERT GILDART

Hikers passing through a spruce-fir community are likely to be surprised by a mottled dark gray or brown bird with a conspicuous black face, throat, and chest patch—that shows absolutely no fear of the hikers' approach. Upon seeing the bird, hikers are further surprised to find that if they walk toward it, the bird may do nothing more than circle a nearby tree. If charged, the bird may fly to an overhanging branch, but seldom will it fly away, although it does possess excellent powers of flight. Meet the spruce grouse, which apparently feels so secure in the depths of its surroundings that it may let you approach to within arm's length. There are documented cases of people who have reached out and picked the bird up from its perch. Because of its total lack of fear, this wilderness grouse has earned the nickname "fool hen." But spruce grouse is a better name, for it prefers spruce trees, the needles of which provide one of its staple foods. Other requirements are abundant huckleberry plants, insects for its young, and sparse groundcover. They may play some role in propagating huckleberries by eating the fruit and then passing the seeds.

Male spruce grouse. BERT GILDART

Alpine Tundra

The alpine zone is perhaps the most spectacular, with its glacier-carved peaks and ridges, and its annual riot of wildflowers. It is characterized by the absence of trees, instead offering a toehold to cushion plants such as phlox, snow cinquefoil, and carpet pink and other ground-hugging species. Almost all alpine plants are perennials, fit to make the most of the short growing season. Some, like arctic bellflower, are also found in Greenland and on Ellesmere Island in the high Arctic. Glacier's alpine zone is rocky and steep, so plants mostly grow in isolated pockets and among scattered nooks and crannies. A handful of mammals, including the American pika, hoary marmot, wolverine, and mountain goat, boast remarkable adaptations that help them thrive here year-round.

Pika. CHUCK HANEY

Marmot overlooking Glacier National Park. BERT GILDART

Ptarmigan in its summer camouflage. LEU FRID/SHUTTERSTOCK

When winter comes to these high peaks, heavy snows and strong winds drive elk down to the low country and send massive grizzly bears scurrying to their dens for a long nap. In fact, the harsh alpine weather force just about every creature to leave or hide. But always there remains a beautiful, little one-pound bird—the ptarmigan.

I first met this strange bird while cross-country skiing with a ranger friend in Glacier. The temperature was minus 5 degrees Fahrenheit, and the wind was howling across the vast treeless ridge. Both of us were bundled in heavy down coats, warm leather mittens, and thick woolly long johns. All around us, the snowy world seemed a mighty deserted place. But suddenly, not more than a half dozen paces away, scrunched six balls of puffed-up feathers. They were pure white, as white as the snow over which we traveled. It seemed a miracle that we had not passed them by, unseen. Perhaps the flutter of their wings as they scooted deeper into the snow attracted our attention, or maybe it was the black of their eyes and beaks that contrasted so sharply with the endless snow. We wanted a better look and so we moved closer, trying not to startle them. But we need not have worried; fear is not part of their nature, and they only returned our stares as if to say, "Any creature out in this weather must be just another ptarmigan."

The white-tailed ptarmigan, or Lagopus leucurus, is well named. Lagopus means "rabbit foot." Long feathers cover their feet, which do look a lot like rabbit feet. The feathers protect from the cold and also serve as snowshoes, enabling the birds to walk on top of soft, fluffy snow. The species name, leucurus, refers to the white tail. But ptarmigans are camouflaged for all seasons. In spring, the birds molt and through the summer sport feathers mottled in brown, gray, and white. So well do they blend in with the rocks and boulders that an occasional hiker is seriously startled when a lichen-covered "rock" takes flight, cackling and beating its wings as it sails off into the blue.

To stay warm, ptarmigans fluff up their feathers like other birds, but they also conserve heat by taking advantage of the insulating qualities of the snow. They form shelters by diving into the snow and scratching out a hollow, or by pressing their bodies into the soft powder and then letting the wind drifts snow around them. Outside these snow "caves," the windchill may be minus 40 degrees Fahrenheit, but inside it is relatively calm and cozy.

Ptarmigan in its winter coat. SOPHIA GRANCHINHOL/SHUTTERSTOCK

Bighorn rams. BERT GILDART

For many visitors, another alpine denizen, Rocky Mountain bighorn sheep, is almost synonymous with Glacier Park because they are so readily seen on the cliffs above Many Glacier Hotel and Swiftcurrent Motor Inn. During summer, bands of sheep graze the slopes in seeming peace. But during autumn rut, the valley resounds with the cracking blows of horns as rams battle for dominance.

As with bighorn sheep, mountain goats are emblematic of Glacier, in part because the Great Northern Railway, eager to draw passengers to its grand hotel in East Glacier, adopted the goat for its logo and as its mascot. But mountain goats are also a fitting symbol of the park, supremely suited to year-round life on the high peaks. Split hooves with rubbery, high-traction inner pads help them cling to sheer cliffs, and a layer of long, hollow guard hairs over a dense woolly undercoat keeps them warm down to minus 50 degrees Fahrenheit.

Above: *Mountain goat in its winter coat.* CHUCK HANEY

Below: *Mountain goat kids.* BERT GILDART

Whitebark pine. GLACIER NPS

Ghost Forest

Glacier's landscape is a dynamic one, everchanging as mountains erode, streams incise valleys, and the forest blackens from wildfires only to re-green in a succession of plant communities. The weather can shift from sunny skies to sleet or snow and back again in less time than it takes to pull a jacket from your daypack. Wildlife populations, too, fluctuate depending in large part on the abundance or scarcity of food sources.

Often a change in one part of the ecosystem sends ripples throughout the park. Such is the case in the processes we can see unfolding in Glacier's "Ghost Forest" on the Scenic Point Trail, which starts on Two Medicine Road 0.3 mile east of the Two Medicine Ranger Station.

Follow the trail south and east, past Appistoki Falls and onto the ridges leading to Scenic Point. Here you'll find wraithlike trees flanking the trail, dead limber pines, ghostly remnants of a grove that once flourished here. Their story is intimately intertwined with Glacier's wildlife, an exotic fungus, and your own visit to this place.

Three species of white pine are native to Glacier, each favoring different environments. Limber pine *(Pinus flexilis)* grows on the windswept, dry ridges on the park's east side. Western white pine *(Pinus monticola)* is found in the moist montane forests on the western slope. And whitebark pine *(Pinus albicaulis)* endures at the upper limits of the subalpine zone, near timberline.

Being related, all three of these pines are similar in appearance and bear their needles in bundles of five. All three are slow growing but typically long lived, with some specimens in Glacier reaching 700 years in age. They also produce cones rich with seeds, and those seeds, packed with energy, are an important food source for bears, birds, squirrels, and other animals. Scientists say that whitebark pine seeds, for example, are 52 percent fat, 21 percent carbohydrate, and 21 percent protein. One gram (five or six seeds) of fresh, mature seeds provides an average of 7 calories.

Here's where it gets interesting. If five or six seeds contain only 7 calories, a grizzly bear would have to eat huge piles of seeds to pack on the fat needed for its long winter sleep. And, through the hard work of a small, furry intermediary, that's exactly what happens. In years when the cone crop is abundant, red squirrels busily cache thousands of cones and seeds for later use in piles called middens. This behavior coincides with the bears' phase of intensive eating ("hyperphagia"), gorging on any food they can find to prepare for hibernation. When cone crops are abundant, both black and grizzly bears climb to the slopes where white, limber, and whitebark pines grow and then sniff out and raid the squirrels' middens. The seeds are a vital food source—studies show that, when seeds are abundant, grizzly bears may eat nothing else and female bears produce more cubs.

Clark's nutcracker. GLACIER NPS

Clark's nutcrackers also cache pine seeds, anywhere from 30,000 to 100,000 seeds by a single bird in one season. They carry a few dozen seeds at a time in a pouch under their tongues and bury them in the soil or in rock crevices, sometimes flying miles from the source tree. The birds return to these caches in winter to uncover and eat the seeds, a remarkable feat of memory. But not every cache or every seed is recovered, so the nutcrackers' efforts help to disperse the seeds and thereby sow new stands of pine. Ravens also cache the seeds, and other birds such as crossbills and dusky grouse seek out the pines to feed.

Unfortunately, this once-abundant food source and the web of life it supports nearly vanished from the park (and throughout the West). In the early 1900s, a fungus from Asia and Europe, white pine blister rust *(Cronartium ribicola)*, was accidentally introduced to the eastern United States. The fungus forms cankers in the cambium, impeding the transport of water and nutrients up a tree's trunk, eventually killing the tree. Young pines are most susceptible, but mature trees are also afflicted. The subsequent spread of blister rust has reduced populations of limber, whitebark, and western white pine by as much as 90 percent.

In the 1960s, work crews sprayed the pines with antibiotics, hoping to stop the die-off. I worked on one of those crews for almost four years, but sadly our efforts were of little avail.

Today, however, researchers are cautiously optimistic after finding small reservoirs of white pines that are genetically rust-resistant. In 1997, the U.S. Forest Service began collecting seeds from surviving whitebark and limber pines in Glacier and growing seedlings in cooperation with the agency's nursery in Coeur d'Alene, Idaho. Then in the early 2000s, they planted 6,400 whitebark pines and 4,700 limber pine seedlings in the park, including within the Ghost Forest. Although not all the seedlings survived, the program has increased the number of rust-resistant pines.

It's easy to grasp the ecological value of preserving these trees—they're a key component of Glacier's forests, holding soil in place, casting shade and retaining critical moisture, and providing nutrient-rich food for birds, bears, squirrels, and other animals. But there's one more strand in the web of life tethered to these trees: us. Studies show that when pine cone crops are low, grizzly bears tend to forage in places where they're more likely to run into people. Instead of feasting on pine nuts on remote ridges, the bears feed on trailside berry patches, in bottomland meadows, and perhaps even at campgrounds and cabins, drawn by the aroma of human food and garbage. That puts people at risk of an unpleasant bear encounter, which in turn raises the chances that a so-called "problem bear" will have to be put down.

Clearly, once you know what to look for, a visit to the Ghost Forest reveals a story that encompasses much more than spectral limber pines. It's a powerful spot to ponder the interconnectedness of place, plants, animals, and ourselves. And, with luck, you may see an industrious Clark's nutcracker poking in the soil near one of the old trees, planting a seed.

Family Members

Hundreds of different species of wildflowers lift their heads throughout the park's brief summer, and though many appear to be drastically different from one another, looks can be deceiving. Examples include the exquisitely yellow glacier lily and the showy beargrass.

Because of its huge, white, multi-flowered head, the true identity of beargrass *(Xerophyllum tenax)* may at first escape you, but if you examine one of the hundreds of individual flowers comprising the plant's inflorescence, you'll see the species does conform to a unique family formula. Every single one of the tiny flowers has three sepals, three petals, six pistils, and three stamens—it is, in fact, a member of the lily family.

Beargrass, though always blooming somewhere in the park in the summer, tends to be cyclic—blooming at and above timberline when conditions align, about once every seven or eight years. Despite its common name, the plant is not a favorite of bears, but they do munch the tender juicy base of the grass-like leaves upon emerging from hibernation. Then they turn to the underground bulbs of the glacier lily *(Erythronium grandiflorum)*, a glamorous species in its own right.

Beargrass. BERT GILDART

Sticky Geranium. JACOB W. FRANK/GLACIER NPS

Glacier lily. JACOB W. FRANK/NPS

Montropa Uniflora. GLACIER NPS

Glacier lilies usually bloom before beargrass, often emerging along the edge of receding snowbanks. The species may appear as dense mats in extensive fields of brilliant yellow, so the glacier lily can be as conspicuous as its close relative. Also, its specific name, grandiflorum, means, "large-flowered," so it is easy to appreciate the plant when it is in full bloom—or when it is compared with the delicate white flowers of beargrass.

Grouping members of plants together by virtue of family similarities is a good way to learn more about the adaptive and evolutionary capabilities of plants. At least twenty-four other park plants are classified as lilies, including trillium and mariposa lily. Each has found its own niche in the park's vast ecosystem, and though different in outward appearance, all still share the same family formula. That makes some of the more diminutive lilies kissing cousins to the oval-headed beargrass, a species that can reach heights of over three feet and so tower over most of the park's other wildflowers, including all of its other wild lilies.

The Ecosystem View

Not only have Glacier personnel assumed a front role in grizzly bear management, but they've also established themselves as leaders in addressing issues that at first glance may seem to be outside their immediate jurisdiction. Consideration of the larger ecosystem around the park plays an increasing role, and rightfully so, for Glacier National Park is not an island, and management decisions made by other agencies significantly affect the park itself.

One important piece of the Glacier ecosystem is the 200-square-mile Badger-Two Medicine. This extraordinary tract of almost entirely roadless land is flanked on the south by the Bob Marshall Wilderness , on the east by the Blackfeet Indian Reservation, and on the north by Glacier National Park. To the Blackfeet people, it's a sacred place. As stated on the Blackfeet Nation website, the Badger-Two Medicine "is the home of our creation story, and has continued to be a place of refuge and healing for 10,000 years. It provides strength, subsistence, and cultural identity to our people, which is why the Blackfeet Nation has vowed to protect it."

The U.S. Forest Service, however, long supported building roads throughout the area to provide access for oil and gas companies who want to drill there. In 1982, as the agency responsible for managing the area, the Forest Service issued forty-seven oil and gas leases. The Blackfeet Nation contested the leases, saying the agency skipped required consultations with the tribe. Since then, the Blackfeet have successfully fought to prevent drilling in the Badger-Two Medicine. Said Galen Bullshoe, "Our grandfathers went up in the Badger-Two Medicine to fast and sweat. Their spirits are still up there. The elk herds that I hunt up by Goat Mountain would leave if they drilled up there."

In 1989, Glacier's superintendent argued for an ecosystem approach, noting that the Badger-Two Medicine provides an important linkage of "habitat and travel corridors for wildlife that spends a portion of each year in the park." Implicit in his statement was the conviction that the Badger should be managed as a wilderness area, one that could provide significant benefits for wide-ranging wildlife.

Efforts to protect the Badger-Two Medicine have apparently paid off. In March 2009, the Lewis and Clark National Forest formally adopted a travel management plan proposed by the Blackfeet Nation that favors traditional non-motorized uses in the Badger-Two Medicine and prohibits motorized use on more than 200 miles of trails. Finally, in June 2020, the U.S. Court of Appeals upheld a decision to cancel the last oil and gas lease in the area. That same month, the Blackfeet Nation announced draft congressional legislation to permanently protect the Badger-Two Medicine as a Cultural Heritage Area.

In 1977, UNESCO designated Glacier as a World Biosphere Reserve. This recognized the value of Glacier National Park's ecological resources for both conservation and scientific work. Such a designation means that park managers must maintain watchful eyes toward surrounding development. Oil and gas exploration on adjacent lands threaten wildlife, habitat integrity, quietness, solitude, and water quality, and the park's naturally functioning ecosystems.

Recognizing that no single jurisdiction has the mandate or resources to address regional environmental issues, Glacier's managers have joined others in what is known as the Crown Managers Partnership that embraces an ecosystem concept known as the "Crown of the Continent," referring to an 18-million-acre region extending from south of the Bob Marshall Wilderness through Glacier National Park and north into southern British Columbia and Alberta. Officials from federal, tribal, provincial, and state land and resource management agencies meet regularly and work together to coordinate policies, monitor environmental conditions, and educate one another and other landowners on issues facing the ecosystem. The partnership's key programs include protecting and restoring limber and whitebark pine stands, stopping the spread of invasive species on

Above: *Westslope cutthroat trout.* GLACIER NPS

both water and land, preserving habitat and ensuring the resiliency of westslope cutthroat trout and bull trout populations, and improving the management of large carnivores, with a focus on grizzly bears.

Above: *Cleaning watercraft to stop the spread of aquatic invasive species (AIS) harmful to native bull trout populations.* GLACIER NPS

Over the years, other management and conservation efforts have addressed a variety of threats to Glacier's wildlife and wildlands. Fisheries managers keep a wary eye on mining and logging operations in British Columbia that could harm the North Fork of the Flathead River, which flows along Glacier's western boundary and is a prime spawning stream for native bull trout, listed as a species of concern in Montana. Meanwhile, invasive zebra and quagga mussels, carried on boats and other watercraft, have spread into Montana. The mussels threaten native fisheries, can clog pipes and other water infrastructure, and may even overtake rocky shorelines, creating an unnatural, sharp-shelled, smelly mess. All watercraft are required to undergo inspection before entering park waters. Park managers have also temporarily closed some waters to boating as needed to prevent mussel infestations.

Another threat to Glacier's tranquility and possibly its wildlife is the number of low-flying sightseeing helicopter and airplane tours. The noise and mere presence of such flights detract from Glacier's wilderness qualities, and research indicates wildlife may be adversely affected. In the fall of 2021, the park announced a draft air tour management plan that would limit the number of flights and eventually phase them out altogether.

WILDFIRES

Another issue that has little regard for park boundaries is fire. Large wildfires swept through Glacier in 1910, the same year that it was designated as a national park, and fire has always been a natural force in shaping the region's forests. In fact, fires have burned within Glacier's boundaries in every year since its establishment as a park, with the exception of 1964. Many species, such as lodgepole pine, huckleberries, and native grasses, depend on fire to clear undergrowth and release nutrients back into the soil. In this way, fire plays a vital role in forest and grassland succession, helping to create an everchanging patchwork of habitats for wildlife.

Unfortunately, decades of fire suppression and a warming climate have led to wildfires that are larger, more intense, and harder to fight. On September 7, 1988, a fire started by lightning in the adjacent Flathead National Forest crossed the North Fork of the Flathead River into Glacier National Park and eventually burned a total of 27,000 acres. Called the Red Bench Fire, it destroyed twenty-eight homes and several outbuildings, including several historic structures built in the 1920s at Polebridge. It collapsed the bridge over the North Fork, warping its steel girders with extreme heat.

Experts agreed that prevailing conditions minimized the chances of stopping the fires of 1988 throughout the West. Red Bench was no exception. Fanned by 40-mile-per-hour winds, within hours it burned hundreds

Burned forest at night. KEVIN LEAGUE

of acres. When the smoke cleared, there was one pleasant surprise: The historic Polebridge Ranger Station, thought to have been lost in the fire, remained standing, as did several other buildings in the burned area

A similar scenario unfolded in 2017, when on August 10 lightning stuck in timber on the north side of Sprague Creek, east of Lake McDonald Lodge. The resulting Sprague Fire gradually grew over the next three weeks until, on August 31, it exploded, doubling in size thanks to strong winds and extremely dry conditions. Despite heroic efforts by firefighters, the blaze destroyed the dormitory building at the historic Sperry Chalet; only the stone walls remained standing. (The nearby dining hall was spared, and the dormitory was rebuilt, reopening to guests in July 2020.) Before being quenched by winter snowfalls, the Sprague Fire burned nearly 17,000 acres, closing Lake McDonald Lodge and the western half of Going-to-the-Sun Road, smothering the McDonald Valley in smoke, and leading to evacuation warnings in Apgar Village and portions of West Glacier.

Although many viewed the Red Bench and Sprague Fires as tragedies, park managers consider lightning-started fires to be natural events. Gary Gregory, a resource management specialist, said, "The forest will burn, but it is a natural process that is part of the way that forests stay healthy. Fire creates much of the diversity that makes the park so interesting." Park managers say that we have just begun to understand the importance of fire as a natural part of the forest and grassland ecosystems.

Clements Hanging Gardens. CHUCK HANEY

Annuals and Perennials

For nine to ten months they lie dormant: plants that show no flowering life and exist only as seeds, roots, tubers, or underground stems. Should you dig one up and look at it all covered with mud, it would appear lifeless. But in the tenth or eleventh month, changes begin to occur. Tiny structures emerge—hypocotyls, epicotyls, and cotyledons. These are the predecessors of roots, stems, and leaves, the plant's nutrient storehouses.

By the end of the tenth month (perhaps around the middle of June), snows have receded, and the duration of daily sunshine is at its greatest. Then these tiny structures shoot outward and upward, as much as an inch a day in some species.

By the end of July, tiny buds unfurl, and soon these plants, which for a time were drab and difficult to identify, sparkle with color and distinctive characteristics. They bounce in the wind, roll across the plains, and tingle as morning zephyrs waft across their faces. For a brief moment, when measured against the course of a year, they add a multiplicity of hues and forms to the park's meadows at every elevation.

Yarrow, fleabane, potentilla, cinquefoil, spirea, crazyweed, and lupine are a few of the 1,000 or so species growing in the park.

Above: *Cinquefoil.* JACOB W. FRANK/NPS
Below: *Yarrow.* GLACIER NPS

Some of these plants are annuals, or species that complete their lifecycle in one year and then die. They produce seeds that carry on the next generation. In contrast, perennials persist from one year to the next, sprouting anew from the same root. Perennials dominate in the alpine zone because the growing season is too short for most annuals to complete their lifecycle.

All of the emerging plants serve some function in the overall ecosystem: binding soil in place, providing nectar for hungry insects, offering forage for grazing animals, and more. The perennial sticky geranium, for example, is a major food for elk and deer in spring and summer. Black and grizzly bears also eat geraniums. Look for its five rosy-purple petals atop an erect stem with deeply lobed green leaves covered with sticky, glandular hairs.

For scientists, cinquefoil, which blooms throughout summer, is an indicator species. This perennial isn't a preferred item on the menu of deer and elk, but they'll eat it if better forage isn't available. When wildlife biologists find nibbled cinquefoil, they know that the range is being overgrazed.

Yarrow, a perennial forb with showy white flowers on tall, slender stems, is mildly toxic but used medicinally by local tribes. For generations, the Blackfeet have sipped yarrow tea to relieve coughs, sore throats, and nausea.

Some years see a bumper crop of wildflowers, while in other years they may be less abundant. The difference likely lies in the vagaries of spring snowmelt and rains, followed by summer sunshine. Summers here can sometimes be cool and cloudy, with less solar energy for plants. But when conditions are right, wildflowers paint Glacier's coulees, slopes, and meadows with every color imaginable.

Above and below: *Scientists measuring the terminus of Grinnell Glacier. Recording this data is critical to understanding the impacts of global climate change on Glacier National Park.* GLACIER NPS

CLIMATE CHANGE AND GLACIER'S FUTURE

SINCE 1880 AND THE START OF THE INDUSTRIAL REVOLUTION, the average global temperature has risen 2 degrees Fahrenheit, with two-thirds of that increase occurring since 1975. Although 2 degrees F. may not seem like much, a tremendous amount of heat is needed to warm all of the planet's oceans, the atmosphere, and the land surface by that much. Bear in mind that a 1- to 2-degree drop was all that was needed to plunge the Earth into the Little Ice Age, and a 5-degree drop resulted in the last great continental glacial period, which lasted 10,000 years.

The amount of warming alone is not the only concern. The pace of warming—the speed at which temperatures are rising—also spells trouble. As the world heats up, quickly, many species will not be able to adapt fast enough to survive.

Finally, some regions of the planet are warming even more than others. In fact, Glacier National Park is warming at nearly double the global average. Summer highs over 90 degrees Fahrenheit, once rare here, are occurring more frequently, and warm weather (and fire season) comes earlier in the spring and lingers later in the fall.

Park visitors can see and feel the effects for themselves. The park's mountains once held eighty glaciers, defined as an icefield larger than twenty-five acres. By 2005, only thirty-two glaciers remained. And many park visitors are disappointed when they arrive only to find diminished views, poor air quality, and closed trails and roads due to wildfires and smoke, the result of drought- and disease-stressed forests, a longer fire season, and more intense wildfires.

Many effects are more subtle but no less troubling. Visitor numbers have increased overall and also into the "shoulder" seasons in spring and fall as milder weather prevails. It is harder to find a time when roads, parking lots, and trails aren't crowded. Warmer water in streams is helping to spread a native freshwater algae, Didymosphenia geminata, commonly known as didymo or rock snot. Nuisance blooms form thick mats that coat streambed rocks, hampering fish spawning and making them slippery for waders. Shorter winters mean a potentially longer growing season for alpine wildflowers but less water available for plant uptake. Already, studies started in the 1980s have documented a significant decline in many alpine plant species. Declines have also been seen in ptarmigan numbers. Biologists worry that mountain goats, wolverines, and pikas will also struggle to adapt to a warmer world.

Reversing global temperature trends will require global solutions, but local efforts can play a role. Glacier National Park has installed solar panels to provide power at several visitor centers and ranger stations, and a micro-hydropower unit provides electricity at Goat Haunt. The park also encourages visitors to do their part. Turn vehicles off rather than letting engines idle. Leave your car and ride the free park shuttle on Going-to-the-Sun Road. Walk or bicycle for short trips and errands. When you return home, consider reducing your heating and cooling needs, drive less, buy locally produced foods and other goods, and reduce, reuse, and recycle.

North Fork of the Flathead River. KEVIN LEAGUE